Thomas Shepard Goodwin

The Natural History of Secession

Or, despotism and democracy at necessary, eternal, exterminating war

Thomas Shepard Goodwin

The Natural History of Secession
Or, despotism and democracy at necessary, eternal, exterminating war

ISBN/EAN: 9783337402778

Printed in Europe, USA, Canada, Australia, Japan

Cover: Foto ©ninafisch / pixelio.de

More available books at **www.hansebooks.com**

THE
NATURAL HISTORY
OF
SECESSION;
OR,
DESPOTISM AND DEMOCRACY AT NECESSARY, ETERNAL, EXTERMINATING WAR.

BY
THOMAS SHEPARD GOODWIN, A. M.

"The Union : it must and shall be preserved."
Andrew Jackson.

"Down with the traitor, and up with the stars."
Battle Cry.

NEW YORK:
JOHN BRADBURN (Successor to M. Doolady),
49 WALKER STREET.
CINCINNATI : RICKEY & CARROLL, 73 WEST FOURTH STREET.
BOSTON : A. WILLIAMS & CO., 100 WASHINGTON ST.
1864.

GEO. C. RAND & AVERY,
STEREOTYPERS AND PRINTERS, 3 CORNHILL, BOSTON.

PREFACE.

Some things to human view are accidents. The place they fill in any general system of things, and the assistance they render in any general process of advancement, are not discernible to human scrutiny.

To some minds almost all things, except their own individual existence, interests, and whims, are accidents, at least, not to say nuisances, that ought to be abated. They cry out with the same impetuous vehemence against the insect that disturbs their after-dinner repose, and against a league of traitors sworn to destroy the last remnant of their country's government or perish in the effort.

About an equal amount of plausible persuasion would be required in the case of the insects or of the traitors, to induce this class of persons to cease their opposition to the outrage committed, and even to join in inflicting the like annoyance on their neighbors.

Perhaps it is not an unlawful or unworthy aim to rid this class of the company of some who properly belong not to its number; and to do something in the present emergency of our country's affairs to counteract the mischievous action of such of that number as remain.

In ability for mischief, next superior to those who have no general system and are capable of comprehending none, stand the class who reason fallaciously or from false premises on matters of practical political importance. It

is hoped that individuals of this class will find in the present treatise a fairness, thoroughness, and reliability of argument which will commend itself to their respect, and,
eventually, to their confidence, so far as they are sincere
searchers after truth that they may act on it.

The third and last class with whom the writer views
himself as dealing is composed of those of greater or less
ability of reasoning and sincerity of heart, either within
or without the boundaries of the loyal States, who have
become unconsciously but hopelessly impressed in favor
of political sentiments and doctrines inimical to the existence and well-being of Popular Government. That this
class is both prominent and numerous among us, every
day's inscriptions on the page of history verify. Of them
the present writer asks no favor, no forbearance. If they
are to triumph, he consents to die; and he does not propose to himself to go down to physical or political obliv-
ion in silence or unavenged.

But Popular Government is not an accident in this
world's affairs. It entered prominently into the original
plan. From the dawn of Creation's morning, provision
began to be made for its advent. An ancient prophet of
God divulged the time of its coming, and declared that
"it should stand forever."

It is to be not only perpetual but universal. All the
institutions of ancient monarchy are to be "broken in
pieces and consumed" before it. It came not forth at the
war of the American Revolution, to glitter for a time
with delusive brightness and then go out in the night of
universal despotism which prevailed before. It has not
arisen and prevailed on this continent for three-quarters
of a century, dispensing unparalleled benefits to those
who have been the subjects of its mild, munificent sway, to
sink irrecoverably before the first infuriate combination of

home-born and foreign despots that should league together for its destruction. The world's great Governor has not brought forth this antidote for all the ills of human tyranny, to bless the nations for a little while, and then become extinct through the absence of those qualifications for leadership which can be acquired only in a despotic state of society.

Such are the convictions under which the following pages have been written; and they are presented to the public, not without belief that they will contribute to impart to others a measure of the same deep-rooted and considerate faith in the worth, the necessity, the perpetuity of Free Government in which they have been written, and the same calm purpose to sustain its institutions, or perish when they fall.

That the present century is one of unexampled advancement and celerity of progress in all that pertains to the more useful arts and sciences, is obvious to every one. That this advancement and accelerated progress are due to the relaxation or abridgment of dictatorial rule, is one of those great truths which are gradually making themselves felt and admitted without the puny aid of human logic.

Both the celerity of general movement peculiar to the present age, — which leaves not time for tardy History to perfect its lessons, — and also the exigencies of the new form of civil government that has arisen to fill the place of departing monarchy, demand and justify the present attempt to bring the light of historical reflection to the aid of those on whom devolves the responsibility of defending, not only our existing government, but the very governmental genus to which it belongs, from the fierce and unportended perils that now assail them. And

1*

yet so brief and recent is the period in which historic
Democracy is to be found, that any writing of reflections
upon it must needs approximate to the writing of current
history.

The studies incident to preparing a previous and yet
unpublished volume on the Passing Away of Monarchy
conferred on the present author some preparedness to
treat the topics presented in the following pages. This
preparedness was augmented by thirty years alternate
residence in different sections, north and south, enabling
him, while familiar with the views and mental habits
peculiar to either section, so far to rid himself from the
controlling influence of these peculiarities as to be able
to speak with historic fairness of them both.

The time occupied in the production of the following
pages was the intervals of professional business during
the first two and a half years of war for suppressing the
Secession conspiracy. The date of writing is sometimes
introduced for the purpose of referring to events then
passed, in illustration of views presented.

During the time which has thus elapsed, many of the
practical political positions with which the author set out,
and which were then comparatively new and strange,
have been extensively adopted by the people and put into
operation by the government. While thus much of the
novelty of the work will have been lost, this loss will
have been measurably compensated by the increased
appreciation by the public mind of the importance of
the topics of which it treats.

Most of the time spent in the preparation of the work
has been devoted to attaining the greatest degree of con-
densation compatible with clearness, in order, as far as

practicable, to bring its contents within the reach of that large and increasing class of men among us whose habitual readings approximate the limits of telegram.

That the perpetuity of domestic slavery is compatible with the perpetual coexistence of free government on the same soil, is an opinion that has been very generally attributed to the founders of this government, as generally entertained by the people of the country, until a recent period, and is still entertained by the great majority of the people, if we take the whole country into consideration. By historical argument, and by argument drawn from first principles, to confute an opinion that is sustained by so sage and so universal authority, and in practical politics to take a position antagonistic to the principles on which the government of the country has been conducted from its origin, is thought to be a matter of such gravity as to demand minute, elaborate accumulation in the argument by which that position is sustained.

"To see ourselves as others see us," implies the possession of a grace with which our natures are so sparingly endowed, that producing an accurate portraiture of one's self, or even of our government and national peculiarities, is no easy task. To the difficulty arising from this source, add the immature and undeveloped state of that type of government which is succeeding to the place of decrepid and departing monarchy, a type of which our own government is perhaps the only reliable specimen, and the resulting accumulation of difficulties may perhaps excuse any lack of scientific clearness of arrangement that appears in the matter of the following pages. It is no ignoble achievment to present well some features of a subject that still remains too imperfect or obscure to be entirely grasped, or perfectly portrayed; leaving it for time and a subsequent effort or author, to finish what has only been well begun..

To the unliterary character of the Southern people, or to their modesty, it appears to be due, that the religionists of the North have never enjoyed to any considerable extent the benefit of their criticism. The decision of one of their superior judges, to the effect that a disbeliever in future rewards and punishments was not competent to testify in their civil courts, is a true index of a sentiment almost universally prevalent among them, different from what obtains at the North, and which has seldom been expressed.

In the following pages the apparent ignoring of the minor republics of the present and former days, results, partly from convenience in conducting the argument, and partly from the necessity of regarding the United States as alone responsible for maintaining the cause of civil Liberty before confronting monarchies, and not from any disposition to undervalue those bright but less potent heralds of the day of universal freedom from civil despotism.

The violently agitated current of passing events, with the felt pressure of its enormous perils, must bring into occasional use and justify expressions of unwonted energy; such as would have been objectionable in times of prolonged quiet, and used respecting events of only ordinary interest, or importance. The same circumstances will be found to induce, if they do not justify, a trifling expansion of the English language, by sometimes making use of words, the admissibility of which rests on but very recent authority.

That no more time is at his disposal for perfecting the style and diction of the volume is matter of regret to

THE AUTHOR.

CONTENTS.

CONTENTS.

XV.

XVI.

XVII.

XVIII.

XIX.

XX.

XXI.

XXII.

XXIII.

XXIV.

XXV.

XXVI.

XXVII.

XXVIII.

XXIX.

XXX.

XXXI.

XXXII.

XXXIII.

CONTENTS.

XLV.

XLVI.

XLVII.

INTRODUCTION.

A KING of ancient Babylon, during a recess in the expeditions of his conquering armies, and with the known world almost entirely subjected to his sway, was meditating on the perpetuity of his dynasty, and disposed to ask, "What should be thereafter?" This inquiring disposition of the king, the God of Heaven was pleased to gratify.

Language is always changing to adapt itself to the events, the minds, and modes of thought peculiar to each varying age. Hence it is always lame in describing future events. And as the matter to be communicated was of importance to those who should live by several thousand years remote from the peculiarities of the then current age, an allegorical image was presented in a dream, to convey the desired intelligence. "Its brightness was excellent, and the form thereof terrible. Its head was of fine gold; its chest and arms of silver; its belly and thighs of brass; its legs of iron; and its feet part of iron and part of clay. A stone was cut out without hands, which smote the image on its feet, and brake them to pieces. Then was the iron, the clay, the brass, the silver, and the gold, broken in pieces together, and became like the chaff of the summer threshing-floor, and the wind carried them away that no place was found for them; and the stone that smote the image became a great mountain, and filled the whole earth."

A faithful prophet of God was near, who explained the head of gold to represent the king's own Babylonish empire; the chest and arms of silver to represent the Medo-Persian empire, which succeeded it; the next section of brass to represent the Macedonian empire which succeeded the Medo-Persian; and the legs of iron he interpreted to represent the base military strength of the Roman empire. Thus we have presented the whole of historic monarchy, practically complete, and left standing on its conglomerate feet and toes, which appear to represent the modern kingdoms of Europe and Western Asia, into which the dual Roman empire dwindled down; when, suddenly, a principle, antagonistic to all monarchy, developed itself without human design or shaping, smote the hoary structure on its feet, and the whole historic embodiment crumbled, became contemptible, and passed practically out of existence.

While monarchy remains anywhere extant and dominant, those ancient empires, though long since passed from the plane of physical existence, still stand, to uphold the prestige of their kind, and send a powerful sanction from the distant past, and a moulding influence, to fashion and sustain the latest and feeblest of their degenerate progeny. But when the impinging force of a developed form and principle, hostile to all monarchy, breaks in pieces the only remaining representatives of that kind of government, then, not only the conglomerate residuum impinged upon, but the ancient and perfect, and yet influential specimens of the order may with propriety be said to break and crumble together; and, as a class and kind of government, to become powerless and contemptible as chaff, while their newly-developed antagonist enlarges, to fill their place. This antagonist can be no other than our American self-government; and dates and numbers accompanying the prophetic declaration of its universal spread, as well as the marked character of recent national changes in every part of the world, point to about the present century as the time of its gradual establishment and spread.*

Though the above views of prophecy suggest the arrangement of the matter which the following pages contain, it is only the historic verity of what is here taken into view that is relied on in support of any of the conclusions thought to be maintained.

---

* See *Lectures on Prophecy*, by George Junkin, D. D. Carter. Philadelphia: 1844. To these Lectures the writer listened while an undergraduate of Miami University, over which institution Dr. Junkin at that time presided.

2*

NATURAL HISTORY OF SECESSION.

I.

THE greatest secular event of this or of any
other age, is the transfer of the reins of civil
power to the many, from the few.

Among the strangest capabilities and habits
of man — the most versatile of created beings —
is the capability and habit of submitting to the
dictation of his fellow-man. This forms the only
foundation on which monarchy can rise or rest.
When and wherever this ceases to exist, then
and there — and then and there only — will monarchy or despotic civil authority be known no
more.

Among the great facts of human history,
nothing that was destined to decline ever displayed more of vastness and perpetuity than

civil monarchy. From the days of Nimrod down to the year of grace, 1776, hardly anything appeared to intimate that division into the two hitherto inevitable classes — slave and master, subject and sovereign — was not the normal and necessary condition of the race. Crowned with the Babylonish empire as its "head of gold," monarchy, through successive ages of universal prevalence, had wrought itself into an august embodiment that promised to absorb within itself all that remained of human history. The antagonistic civil principle had not yet germinated. The "little stone" that was to "become a great mountain, and fill the earth" instead, had not yet been "cut out without hands." And yet there was a progressive degeneracy in that which constituted the peculiar richness and excellence of monarchical power. Through the Medo-Persian and Macedonian ages, this degeneration progressed, until the iron despotism of the Roman empire, and its representatives and successors, the modern kingdoms of Europe and western Asia, displayed the once glorious and beneficent principle of civil monarchy in forms of baseness and cruelty unsurpassed by anything outside the confines of the darkest barbarism.

---

*The reference here is to the prophet Daniel, who is interpreted as saying that monarchical government must become extinct at about the present age of the world.

Perhaps the basis of monarchical strength — the capability and easy habit of submitting to dictation — had been gradually ebbing out of the popular masses, thus necessitating the assumption of harshness and violence on the part of the ruling few, in order to save their inherited or usurped preëminence from falling into hopeless desuetude.

The word monarchy, when strictly defined, describes the condition of affairs in which one man presides in supreme civil power over the state or nation. In common usage, the word is understood to apply to *all* those modifications of the one-man-power which fall short of democracy. In democracy the majority rule. The word despotism describes an intense, abused form of monarchy.

As monarchy is founded on nothing but the ability and habit of the people to submit to the dictation of superiors, so democracy is founded on nothing but the opposite of this, namely, the permanent inability of the people to submit to the dictation of any but themselves.

These two plans or principles of government are intensely antagonistic: so much so, that wherever they exist together, annihilating war is inevitable, in one form or another, until the one principle or the other is extirpated.

Such being the state of the case, and monarchy being already universal in the Old World, where should a place be found, whereon to develop the germ of free government? This inquiry would have been a serious, perhaps an unanswerable one, had not the wise and gracious Ruler of the universe, from the first founding of the world, reserved the American continent for this special purpose.

· As the age drew near in which monarchy was to become extinct, two great preparatory operations were found to be going on. First, the continent was being discovered, explored, and rendered accessible and habitable. Secondly, a race of men, the first of the nations, were being trained, separated, and at last transported thither, among whom the principle of popular self-government was to be planted, developed, and strengthened into unconquerable prevalence.

II.

WHILE the continent that had been reserved for the birthplace of civil freedom was yet an undiscovered wilderness, roamed over only by a few tribes of feeble savages, the race of men that were to be its first fit occupants were being thus prepared.

An island was selected in the temperate zone, best fitted for the development of mental, moral, and physical strength, remote alike from the stinting cold and poverty of the frigid, and from the sickening, passion-kindling, heat of torrid, latitudes; sufficiently near the continent to admit the stimulating influence and intercourse of the European society of nations; sufficiently isolated to remain largely uninfluenced by the degeneracy and turmoils of those nations. Here the aboriginal inhabitants were crossed by an admixture of the civilized and all-conquering Romans, and afterward successively by four other of the most stalwart races of middle and

23

northern Europe.   The result was, a people more vigorous and controlling than any contemporaneous nation of the earth.   Their vigor displayed itself in an early separation from the Romish Church, and a successful defiance of both its corruptions and its force.

The despotism that prevailed oppressively over the rest of Christendom was soon broken and permanently modified in England by the turbulent exactions of the nobility.   The "Magna Charta," exacted by his nobles from King John, is justly regarded as the first distinct germ of modern free government.

This turbulent nobility at length destroyed itself in its intestine wars, and left the Commons — the elected representatives of the common people — to rise into an importance which they have never resigned, and which is as great, perhaps, as is compatible with the continued existence of monarchy.

From a people thus prepared and trained — a people of mental and moral stature, and national strength and resources second to none of its contemporaries — were selected the chosen few who were to plant the first permanent settlements on the continent that had been reserved to be the birthplace and heritage of popular government.   Here they hardened under un-

wonted trials and privation, removed by a
voyage of months from the efficient presence of
that government under whose ample protection,
and from the enlightened community in whose
affluent bosom, they had been reared. Exposed
to the rigors of a trying climate, assaults of savages, the ravages of disease, and in no slight
degree to the perils of starvation, they gradually
became aware of their ability to protect themselves, and became insensibly possessed of a
mysterious inability to submit to needless and
unreasonable dictation. Gradually reinforced in
numbers from the source from which the original
settlers sprang, there resulted a homogeneous
and unique national character, one great essential of which was the yet latent but inexorable
necessity of self-government.

8

III.

Two permanent settlements were made in North America at about the same period, and a few hundred miles apart. One at Plymouth, Massachusetts, by a religious community, brought out from its former home by the pressure of religious restrictions, to find more perfect religious freedom. The other at Jamestown, Virginia, by a secular community, moved by the motives which ordinarily prompt to the colonizing of new countries, — a desire to promote national enlargement, and to better the condition of the individuals concerned. Each colony drew to itself kindred material from the mother land, and spread. Other settlements, less distinct in character, came to the intervening and adjacent space, amalgamated with either of the first two settlements, and the country, for hundreds of miles in every direction, became compactly filled. The originally secular community became more religious, and the originally religious community gradually became substantially secular, until, to the eye of the common observer, no lineament of the original diversity of germ was discernible in the homogeneous product of the two primal settlements. Whether a century of amalgamated existence and united governmental activity has or has not eradicated original incongruities of character from the offspring of these separate germs, is a question that has been clothed with momentous importance by the events of 1861-2.

The original religious difference between the Northern and Southern colonies, though diminished, has never become extinct. The activity of Northern minds still takes a religious turn. What there is among them of real faith in God and in his revealed Word assumes a more positive, aggressive, and fruitful type than elsewhere; and what there is among them of ungodliness and infidelity assumes, to a very remarkable extent, a sanctimonious aspect and a religious form. Whole denominations of churches keep up the costly rites and ceremonies of religious worship, merely to clothe themselves with the external decorum of believers, to give expression and exercise to those religious faculties and feelings common to the race, to emphasize

their rejection of revealed truth, and to retain
their followers from being drawn under the
dominion of an evangelical faith. While in the
South, real religion is more silent and retiring,
and ungodliness prides itself on the frank and
open bearing of the undisguisedly profligate.

Diversity of climate and other accidents have
induced more or less difference of character and
habit between the descendants of the Northern
and Southern colonists, in addition to any diversity that originally marked their ancestors. All
these, with the original and continued religious
difference that existed and still exists, may serve
to induce diversity of social tastes, and even a
degree of antipathy between the dwellers in
the Northern and Southern portions of the
Union; but all this sinks into utter non-impor-
tance in the presence of the one great characteristic feature of the age. Despotism and
Democracy have for years been mustering their
adherents for deadly and final conflict; and by
the all-absorbing power and importance of this
struggle, where it is present, any other shade or
ground of difference between two civil communities is merged at once in oblivious insignificance.

The question, then, whether, between the
people of the Northern and Southern portions

of the Union there exists such radical divergence of character as necessitates the sundering of the civil ties that hitherto united them, becomes simply the question whether the people of these two sections have become arrayed on different sides in the great strife that is going on throughout the civilized world between the friends and the enemies of popular self-government.

If both are on the same side in this one great, all-important, all-absorbing, conflict of the age, then any present or partial difference that may separate them on minor points will of necessity soon subside and disappear, and leave them naturally and substantially united. If, on the contrary, the people of these two sections are fairly and permanently fixed on different sides in the great conflict of the age, then, no act of separation, no peace-treaty or covenant, no guaranty or mediation, can prevent their warring with deadly animosity, until one or the other party to the strife is converted or consumed.

3*

IV.

With regard to the position of the Northern States, on the great question of the day, there is, and can be no difference of opinion. If their own profession, and the admission of all foreign nations, that they are the peculiar possessors, advocates, and champions, of free government, were not satisfactory proof on this point, their peculiar follies and weaknesses, as displayed in the conduct of the present war, their apparent utter inability to have a governing policy, or an efficient head, should establish beyond a cavil that they are anything else but monarchists.

The fact of the Northern States having abolished slavery within their borders is some proof of the depth and genuineness of their professed democracy, inasmuch as the causes which induced this line of action, and the action itself, would have tended somewhat strongly to induce and to confirm the democratic element. The fact that the people of the Northern States have never exacted from their several States, nor from the general

30

government, distinct admission of the citizenship of their colored population, limits, though perhaps it does not go far to countervail, the depth and sincerity of their claims to being considered democratic.

A still more serious limit to the genuineness of these claims is found in the history of the tame submissiveness with which the people and statesmen of the North, have almost unresistingly accorded a vast predominance of political influence to the Southern minority in the national councils.* This is an error, not of design, but of unconscious feebleness in what forms the basis of all reliable self-government, — an inability to submit to dictation.

Perhaps, on the other hand, some allowance is justly to be made on account of the unorganized, unsuspecting nature of all democratic communities. Only in the presence of a recognized

---

* Out of the seventy-two years of the existence of our government from its organization to the close of Buchanan's administration, Southern men have held the seat of chief executive forty-eight years — just two-thirds of the time. Add to this, that Pierce and Buchanan, two of the Northern Presidents were notoriously mere tools of the South, and owe their elections to that fact, which the history of their administrations never contradicted, — then allow that all offices of emolument and trust under the general government, domestic and foreign, civil, military, and naval, have been distributed to Southerners in approximately the same ratio in which they have held the post of chief executive, — and the result will be a somewhat serious drawback on the validity of the profession of Northerners to being a democratic people.

antagonist is there anything to inspire them
with suspicion, to force on them that organization, or train them to that reconnoitring alertness, from which they naturally lapse in time of
peace. and without which they are defenceless
as sheep.

A monarchical government so readily assumes
the attitude and armament of war that war may
almost be said to be its normal state. Its single
or naturally - united head, always necessarily
vigilant, and alert to maintain its own preëminence in its own community, undergoes but
trifling change of state or activity when it turns
its attention to foes without, or taxes the resources of its realm to resist invasion or to become
itself the invader.

On the other hand, in the democratic community, the law that reduces all preëminence to
the common level — the practical efficiency of
which law is the first condition of democracy —
neutralizes the intelligence and paralyzes the
activity of any one who might be able to warn
of danger, or to direct efforts to forestall disaster,
until such time as the constant aggravation of
prolonged oppression, or some sudden violation
of every sense of justice, rouses the universal
populace with one common purpose to resist.

This natural disposition and tendency of a democratic community to be remiss and inefficient in preserving its rights, and resisting aggression, will account in part for the undue ascendency of Southern influence in our national councils, but it will not wholly account for or excuse this. The historic fact that such notoriously imbecile tools as Frank Pierce and James Buchanan had strong, organized, and in some instances ruling, parties in the North to advocate their election and to sustain their administrations, — is a fact that admits of explanation only on the admission that said parties had become depraved to a great extent of the first essential of democracy, — an inability to submit to usurped dictation.

To extenuate their conduct, it may be said that many of the men who voted to raise these two men to the chief magistracy did so without understanding the import of their deeds. They were practised on by party deceptions; they had been drilled for years to blind submission to party leaders! As much as this can be said in defence of the most grovelling set of slaves that ever fixed upon themselves the shackles of a despot.

The simple truth is, that with more light and

knowledge than ever before illuminated the path
of a people similarly situated, they did what in
them lay, to sell themselves and their country
into the hands of as fierce a set of tyrants as
ever endeavored to usurp the rights of a people
they had purposed to enslave.

V.

CLAIMS OF THE SOUTH TO BEING CONSIDERED DEMOCRATIC
EXAMINED, AND FOUND TO HAVE BEEN SINCERE AT FIRST,
BUT NOW FALSE IN THE EXTREME.

THE people of the Southern States profess also
to advocate, possess, and exemplify the principles
of popular self-government. And it is only by
separating what is fact from what is fiction, in
this profession, that we can arrive at any reliable
conclusion respecting the moving spring of their
rebellion, or the means of bringing our existing
war to a successful close.

That the people of the Southern States, with
comparatively few individual exceptions, sincerely believe themselves to be democratic members
of a democratic community, there can be no
doubt.

But the question before us is not a question
as to what the Southern people believe or suppose themselves to be, or what they are believed
or supposed to be by others. It is a question of
fact, whether they *are* or *are not* capable of themselves exercising or submitting to the exercise
by others, of despotic dictation in civil affairs.

Let the answer to this inquiry be reliably ascertained. and in that answer, and in that only, we have the data for framing a policy which will bring our present grievous intestine war to a successful issue.

The history of the Southern people, at first view, appears to justify the conclusion that their profession of democratic principles is sincere. Originating from the same national stock, transported at about the same period across the same almost interminable ocean (as then navigated), and subjected to the same perils of starvation and savage hostilities. there is nothing wanting but the same severity of climate and poverty of soil, to complete in all essentials the historic parallel between the early experience of the Northern and Southern colonies. Each appears to have had substantially the same experience and training. leading and impelling them to resist the dictatorial exercise of power by the mother country; and with substantially the same result. The end of a century and a half of colonial existence found the accumulated colonies of the North. under the lead of Massachusetts, and of the South, under Virginia. alike prompt and desirous to inaugurate and carry on the war of independence, and alike worthy to share the benefits that war obtained.

Such a test as the war of the Revolution supplied, could not fail to develop any deficiency of
the elements of freedom, had any such deficiency existed at that time.   Since then, the
trade of politicians has been plied in every quarter of the land so thoroughly, so perpetually and
persistently, that any movement of the people
or of any portion of them, requires to be re-
viewed and repeated for some length of time,
before it is safe to consider it as spontaneous or
sincere, and not artificial and produced by demagogues.   But at the time of the Revolution
and before, whatever the people did was reasonably sure to have been done sincerely and of their
own simple motion.   There were tories North
and South; individuals, and sometimes large
neighborhood majorities, who preferred monarchy, or, at least, preferred the old British government, to anything which they thought likely to
be achieved by revolution; and they showed this
preference by active coöperation with the British, or by very obstinate neutrality.   There appears to have been more of these in the extreme
South, than in any other section.   A more enervating climate, less advantages of education, and
of enlarged intercourse, and a more natural indifference as to what government they were under, may account for this.   While the splendid

4

specimens of ability and devotion to Freedom's cause, which were at the same time displayed in the same section, largely offset the other, and almost dispel any suspicion that the Southern colonies, as a section, were behind the North in their demand for national freedom, or in their contributions for its procurement.

The influence which the Revolutionary struggle, with its sacrifices and privations, must have had on those who engaged in it, could not have been other than to deepen and confirm their preference for the cause they espoused, even if that preference had been at first wavering. And the results of the glorious achievements of that war — the sense of triumph, and the rapid rise of national character and wealth — must have overwhelmed the craven spirit of toryism that at first persisted in its preference for British monarchy as its government. Such, we may well believe, was indeed the case. Preferences for monarchical government disappeared. And up to a recent period, almost no one has had the hardihood to avow a preference for any form of government other than the one we have had. So perfectly and so splendidly has the upward progress of our nation exemplified and illustrated the benefits of free government, that evidence amounting almost to proof of hatred to all democracy in the authors of this rebellion, is found in the fact that they have purposed, and are laboring to achieve, the overthrow of this first successful specimen of popular self-government. This government is universally admitted to be the representative and almost the embodiment of all modern free government, and those who are engaged in an assassin struggle for its overthrow are a monstrous anomaly in the world of sequence, if they are not the representatives and champions of the tottering monarchies of a tyrant-ridden world. The gauzy pretence that they are laboring to establish a more perfect form of free government, is but an extorted compliment to the admitted worth and splendor of the one they are laboring to destroy. Nothing else but such pretence could shield them from the open shame of being the common enemies of mankind.

VI.

UNQUESTIONED and unquestionable is the historic record, that, from Washington and Jefferson, down to Marion and Sumter, the Southern colonies supplied many of the bravest warriors of the Revolution, many of the ablest and most devoted of the framers of our present government. Equally certain is it, that the ablest minds of the South, one and all, with sparse exceptions, are now laboring with infuriate zeal to dissipate what the valor of their fathers won, to pull down what the wisdom and devotion of their fathers reared.

This change, that has occurred between the fathers and their sons, demands to be accounted for.

To attribute such a change to caprice, or to political accidents, one or many, without the intervention of the sternest laws, and the deepest principles that influence and govern national character and conduct, would be to abandon all

40

idea of cause and effect in the sphere of man's associate action, and to convert the moral world into a moral chaos, wherein all law is nugatory and reason useless.

That the parties undergoing it should be themselves intelligently cognizant of the change, is not to be expected. It is too deep and radical, its occurrence has been too gradual and silent, it is too total, extensive, and absorbing, to be intelligently comprehended by those who are the subjects of it. It is the greatest and most mysterious change that human character can undergo, next to that change of which the Scriptures say, " as the wind bloweth where it listeth and thou hearest the sound thereof, but canst not tell whence it cometh or whither it goeth, so is every one that experiences it." It is the change from democracy to despotism; or rather the lapse consequent on the conversion from despotism to democracy having been in the first instance imperfect.

When the war of the Revolution was over, and the convention which formed our Constitution had assembled, jarring and repellent interests well-nigh rendered their labors finally abortive.

This was to be expected. Only the heavy

costs of freedom had as yet been proved. The
rich fruits of its possession were still conjectu-
ral; and union, as indispensable alike to their
procurement or preservation, had not then, as
now, become matter of manifold experience.
Sectional interests and even local prejudices
were sufficient to jar, and even repel, the parts
that had not then been formally united, nor
welded into one, by three-fourths of a century
of happy and glorious experience.

No fundamental ground of diversity in principles or practice then displayed itself. Even
the question of slavery was far from being local
at the South. Though the States were all, or
nearly all, slave-holding, the predominance of
interest in that institution was at the South.
Yet the South was far from being unanimous in
favor of slavery; and the North was nearly as
far from being unanimous against it. The leading statesmen of the age, from the South as well
as from the North — themselves slave-holders —
were against perpetuating the institution. They
had successfully perilled their lives, their possessions, and their hopes, to obtain for themselves,
their posterity, and their country, the boon of
civil freedom; and they were then engaged in
the extremely arduous and critical work of giving security and permanence to what their perils,

privation, blood, and toil, had gained. They were deeply conscious of the incongruity of making the perilous and costly consummation of the freedom of one race the occasion of riveting irrevocably the fetters of another race, intermingled among them on the same soil. But the peril of such a course they did not understand. The latent, inevitable, consuming, hostility between despotism and free government, had not, at that early stage of the conflict between these two great principles, been sufficiently demonstrated to be understood. They dreaded only the *usurpations* of those who were despotically disposed; and had no dread of the broader, deeper, and more surely prolific ground of despotism, — the *subservient disposition* of the masses. That the existence of slaves necessitates the existence of masters, and that masters are necessarily tyrants, despots, are truths, obvious enough to us, but which they appear not distinctly to have discovered. The war they had just gone through was looked on as not generically diverse from former wars, and not as the initiatory engagement in a series of conflicts, the most fierce, perhaps, that the world's history will ever have recorded, which are to terminate in the utter subversion of all monarchy.

It was left for us, their descendants, at this

remoter period, by the light which the history
of their day throws forward upon ours, and in
the light which ours and intervening years
throw back on theirs, to discover the truth that
they and we are taking part in the downfall of
universal despotism, the greatest revolution that
civil society ever has been, or will be, called to
pass through; that they and we are fighting
out issues, not for ourselves alone, but for the
human race, — issues not again to be reversed
till the end of time.

Had the patriot framers of the Constitution
of our country's government been permitted to
see and realize the magnitude and extent of
the change they were inaugurating in the world's
history; had they obtained a glimpse of the
inevitable certainty and consuming bitterness of
the wars which they had begun, and which were
to rage at intervals until the last of monarchical
institutions shall have become extinct, sooner
than do as they did, — plant the seeds of inevitable, intestine, consuming war in the bowels of
the sacred structure they were rearing up to be
consecrated to universal Freedom, — such colony
or colonies as refused to pledge themselves to
final emancipation would have been left outside
the Union, till the bitter fruits of their fatal
choice had ripened in destruction on their **own
unpitied heads.**

VII.

HAD the States which persisted in making African slavery perpetual been excluded from the original Union, would the Free United States have prospered as they have done in the union of all the States? The history of the Free States does not admit the shadow of a doubt, that, without any union with, or assistance from, the Slave States, their prosperity would have been great and their advancement irresistible. Their climax of greatness might, perhaps, at no time prior to the present, have reached the point at which it stood when this war began; but there can be no doubt that it would have reached the condition in which it will be found when this war shall close.

The Southern or slave-holding States, on the other hand, would have been early won, to join the prosperous Free States, and abandon slavery, or else they would have become monarchical in form as rapidly as they became so in fact; would

45

have become confederate with European monarchies; and their present war on freedom, would
have taken place ten or twenty years earlier
than it has, and before the Slave States attained
a tithe of their present power for mischief. The
war, in that case, might have been less decisive, more protracted, or repeated at intervals,
more than now, but during its course, whether
long or short, there could hardly have been as
much lying as has been done in Europe and in
the Slave States during each ten days since the
rebellion commenced.

But the truth of the case is, that the patriot
founders of our government never believed that
African slavery, though extant, would become
perpetual. They were themselves possessed of
a love of liberty that outweighed all other considerations. They knew the same sentiment to
pervade their countrymen, North and South.
They knew that the terrible costs of the war
had not only proved the existence and prevalence of this sentiment, but had developed, deep-
ened, and increased the same. They saw with
sanguine faith something of the rich prosperity
that awaited the future of the United States;
and they not unreasonably calculated that this
would confirm the love of freedom in every sec-

tion of the land. And they saw no good reason
to doubt that the evident incongruity of a love
of being free one's self, and the love of enslav-
ing another — the warring difference there was
between the sentiment and the practice of securing the widest liberty to the white, while
imposing the heaviest servitude on the black —
would, at no distant day, while yet the love of
freedom in the citizens was unshaken, eventuate
in the enfranchisement of the slaves.

They secured the *extinguishment* of the *foreign*
slave-trade, and *permitted* the *domestic* slave-trade
to have a free field. They allowed a representa-
tion in Congress to the masters on account of
slaves, and secured the return of the fugitives.
These things they did as a fit and customary
compromise of jarring interests, and left the inevitable opposition between slavery and freedom
to work out the rest; desiring and believing that
the result would be, the ultimate glorious triumph of the latter. Their expectations are not
to be disappointed. But the long delay and
the bloody vale of humiliation, which were to
intervene between the inception and the accomplishment of their hopes, they did not fore-
see. The causes of this partial disappointment
of their expectations, it is worthy of our most
earnest and patient endeavors to understand.

VIII.

THE CONSTITUTION ADOPTED — SLAVERY ABOLISHED IN THE NORTHERN STATES — FROM WHAT INFLUENCES, AND WITH WHAT RESULTS.

THE Constitution, formed by the Convention for that purpose met in Philadelphia, through much difficulty, peril, prayer, and patience, was at length completed. More or less tardily each of the thirteen then existing States gave in its adherence thereto, and on the thirtieth of April, 1789, it went into operation by the assembling of Congress and the induction of George Washington into office as the first President. From this date commenced the progress of the United States in a career of affluence, expansion, respectability, and power, unparalleled and unapproached in the history of nations,* and unchecked, until it was confronted with the product of those seeds of conflict and of dissolution which were planted in the Constitution when

---

* It seems to be only with some qualification that the term nation can be applied to a conglomerate like that which fills the boundaries of our land — a type of population like the gathered nationalities of former universal monarchies, which seems of itself to presage the universal spread of the government they sustain.

its protections of African Slavery were permitted to remain perpetual.

Six of the northernmost of the original thirteen States shed off the incubus of negro slavery without commotion and without regret.

This result was favored by the accident of climate, and perhaps of soil. Negroes are constitutionally adapted to a warm climate. They seem almost incapable of being hardened to a cold climate like the white races. Hence they did not thrive so spontaneously, they did not multiply as rapidly, as in the Southern States; it cost more to keep them, and they were worth less when kept. Again, the bracing climate stimulated both the mental and bodily powers of the white race into greater activity, so that there was less demand for slave labor. The fast-growing spirit of freedom and equality soon produced a social atmosphere in which the individual, if personally otherwise inclined, became deeply ashamed to accept his sustenance or wealth at the hands of an unrequited, half-civilized, half-starved darky. The negro himself became stimulated, if not by the climate, by his large and constant intercourse with intelligent, ingenious, and self-supporting whites, and rapidly and obviously became fit for freedom.

The soil in the Northern States is not suffi-

ciently productive to admit of the constant
production of one great staple crop, to be sold
off for cash; and all experience proves that in
no other circumstances is slave labor profitable.
Nothing but the *potent stimulus* of personal interest will so far overcome the latent inertia of
human powers as to induce a man to apply himself successfully amidst a *variety* of domestic or
agricultural pursuits.   Under a relaxing climate,
authority may avail to impel the slave along in
the deep-worn channel of routine, in the simple
production of cotton, rice, sugar, or tobacco.
But if provisions and teams are also to be raised
as well as the staple crop, the white man will
find it about as cheap to do his work himself, or
to pay some one who will be concerned to save
his varied interests from harm.*   If no great
staple is to be produced at all, if, as is the case
almost throughout the Northern States, affluence
is to spring from the application of skill, industry, and economy, to the multifarious vocations
of a sterile country, slave labor soon proves
itself to be a costly nuisance.

Slavery having been finally and effectually
abolished in the six northernmost of the original
States, and being excluded from the northern-

* See Appendix A at close of volume.

most of the new States which, from time to time, were admitted to the Union, nothing was left in these States to limit or retard the maturing to perfection of the sentiments and principles of free government. "For better for worse," whatever these principles and sentiments lead to was destined here to be witnessed and experienced to its full extent.

Accordingly we see the Northern States preeminent in the increase and general diffusion of wealth and learning; the shipping and manufactures of the country fell almost entirely into their hands, and so well were they handled that history presents no parallel results. Immigration fell so exclusively to the North, that, in 1860, the Northern States possessed two-thirds of the white population of the whole country. The peculiar work of democratic principles — the leveling down of individual preëminence — had at this date been so effectually performed that not only had the Southern oligarchy held control of the general government, and used it for their own purposes for half a century, but when they now came to cast off the Northern States, robbed, insulted, and defied, and these were *compelled* to resort to arms for self-preservation, their armies were like sheep without a shepherd, and their legislature more so. With such a

trembling grasp was power held by their executive, that, at the end of sixteen months of war,
it was not easy to show that they had not injured
themselves by exhaustion, more than they had
inflicted injury on their antagonists ; and Europe
was still in doubt whether the South, with two
men to her one against her in the field, with a
still greater disparity against her in pecuniary
resources and war-material, and without the
shadow of a navy, against the best fleet in the
world, was not destined to have things her own
way, simply by virtue of efficient leadership.

IX.

PRIOR to the adoption of the constitution we have seen that the Southern colonies were settled by a class of men, of character somewhat different from that of the settlers at the North, and for somewhat different purposes. Yet they struck for freedom at the Revolution; they contributed adequately to secure the prize, and shared on terms of equality in the distribution of its benefits. It is true that the contributions from the South toward the achievement of our independence, and the subsequent founding of our government, came more in the form of distinguished leaders than of a reliable or abundant supply of men to fill the army ranks, or a strongly supporting sentiment of the common people. Yet up to the final adoption of the Constitution, and the organization of the government under Washington, we find no ground to justify the suspicion of a radical, even incipient, departure, on the part of the South, from the guidance of the principles of popular government. It is, then, to a period subsequent to the adoption of the Constitution, that we are to look for the inception, growth, and maturing of those principles which have produced the present Rebellion and intestine war. And the first prominent fact that strikes our attention in the search is, that whereas African slavery dwindled to extinction in the Northern States, it progressed uninterruptedly at the South. The causes and the consequences of this progress demand attention, and the latter more than the former. But first the causes.

It is noticeable that in the settlement of the Southern colonies, nobles, or prominent leaders figure extensively. The common people appear not at an early period to have manifested the same power and will to take care of themselves that from the first characterized the colonists of the North. In 1671, in a population of 40,000, Virginia numbered 2,000 slaves and 6,000 indentured white servants; and was presided over by a governor who prayed "that they might long remain free from the pernicious influence of free schools and the printing-press."

The educating trials of colonial experience,

and the salutary discipline of the Revolutionary War, doubtless went far to obliterate aristocratic distinctions, and to make the Southern community in reality what it professed to be, — self-governing by popular suffrage. And yet, neither free schools nor colleges, or other schools not free, nor yet the printing-press, have ever prevailed at the South with more than a tithe of the influence they exerted at the North; and society there has always, to the present time, exhibited strong tendencies to divide itself into dominant and subject classes. This tendency may have had some direct influence in limiting the extension and perfecting of the principles of free government, but it may also be regarded as one strong barrier to the spread of that spirit and practice of emancipation that swept the Northern States.

The warm climate, adapted to the African constitution, made the negroes thrive, and prevented the institution of slavery from declining of its own accord. It also imparted to the master an indolence of disposition, averse to personal application, enterprise, and industry, and went far to reverse those characteristics of the Northern population, which made them scorn alike to become the subjects of another's mas-

tership, or to accept their living at the hands of
slaves over whom they happened to have the
power to extort it.

This indolence of disposition, on the part of
the whites, goes far to account for the absence
of free schools, and the almost entire absence
of a Southern literature to the present day.

The reason why slavery was not abandoned
in the South at the time and under the pressure
of the influence of free institutions for the
whites, which abolished it at the North, is in
no small degree to be found in the fact that the
Southern white population lacked the enterprise
to abolish it, even if the vast majority of them
sincerely desired it to be abolished. The actual
slave-owning part of the Southern white population never has been more than one in thirty.
These hold five-thirtieths of the others, or five
times their own number, identified in interest
with themselves, by blood relationship and family alliance; leaving four-fifths who not only
have no interest in slavery, but whose every
prospect, hope, and privilege, but that of vege-
tating on a scanty subsistence, are blasted by its
presence.

The most prominent of all the causes which
countervailed the abolishing of slavery in the

Southern as it was abolished in the *Northern* States, under the influence of free institutions established for the whites, is, that *the non-slave-holding people of the South lacked the enterprise, intelligence, and daring to demand and exact their democratic rights;* but on the contrary they sat down supinely to the possession of naked existence, under a network of legislation and popular usage which their slave-holding oligarchy had framed for their subjugation. The same is a most prominent cause, without the operation of which, the present nefarious Rebellion against the national government could not have existed two months. And without the subversion of which, this Rebellion can never be put down effectually.*

* In allowing the majority of the people to be defrauded of the right of suffrage in the States that never did, and never could, carry a popular majority in favor of Secession, — as in Virginia, Louisiana, and Tennessee, — and in then permitting these Union majorities to be forced by despotic military power into the armies arrayed against a government which, if left to their choice, they would quite as soon have supported as opposed, the administration of President Lincoln appears to have shown deficiency of aim or an inefficiency of action which ought not to be charged to the account of the necessary weaknesses of democratic government. Perhaps a part of the "damnable inheritance" entailed on the present administration by its immediate predecessor, was the necessity of inaction in this regard; but it appears to be exceedingly desirable to know, whether the constituent of a government on which he is dependent for protection abroad, is or is not entitled to aid from the general executive, when he finds himself in an emergency like that in which these Union majorities were placed. If the only protection to which these Union men were entitled, was to be found in the decisive energy of their own strong arms, under the lead of such men

as could be found in their own number, it might facilitate business very much to have this fact clearly understood, before another such emergency shall arise.

Perhaps no demonstration could be more conclusive that these majorities had become perfectly conformed to the character and condition of the abject many in a despotism than the fact that they allowed — as in Virginia, for instance — the tyrant few, calling to their aid what negro-traders, gamblers and other desperadoes could be collected, to defeat, put down, and immolate, the masses of the community.

X.

Not only did the inertness of character produced by the climate of the Southern States act by deterring the great non-slave-holding majority of white citizens in those States from asserting their rights and enforcing what their interests dictated, in respect to the abolishment of slavery, but the same lack of enterprise also deterred many and many a master from ever acting out his own hearty wish to leave his posterity free from the obvious curse.

Such was the radical working of the despotic principles in the whole framework of society, that it presently became a matter of very great difficulty for a slave to be set free, or for a master to abrogate the onerous prerogatives of ownership.

The fertility of the soil, by enabling the country, for a long time, to bear the embarrening influence of the thriftless institution, contributed far to postpone the day of necessary emancipation.

The number of negroes in the Southern States being much larger than in the Northern, as it was difficult, if not impracticable, to remove them, the apprehended inconvenience of having so large a number of persons of little intelligence or principle, and unused to exercise the rights of freemen, let loose upon a civilized community, operated adversely to emancipation. Perhaps they might have been exported, but the expense and difficulties of the work would have been immense; their labor was needed. The poor whites soon came to prefer poverty and idleness to industry and thrift, and the presence of the slave-system so effectually turned away the immigration of foreign laborers that no one thought of obtaining a supply of labor from that source.

But among all the causes that contributed to withstand the progress of free principles at the South, and to prevent the spread there of that perfect spirit of freedom which cleared the North of slaves, perhaps the most prominent and effectual was the direct influence of so large a proportion of half-barbarous Africans interspersed among them, in forming the character, principles, and habits, of the members of the white community.

It has been before remarked that in these pages we are dealing, not so much with what men suppose themselves to be, or with what they intelligently purpose to do, as we are with what men *are*, from the necessities of the situation in which their ancestors placed them, and in which they consent to remain; and with what they *do*, as a necessary sequence of what they are.

For the " high-born," labor-scorning aristocrat of the South to suppose or to admit that there is anything African in the composition of his character, is not to be expected. And yet, that sparsely-settled white families, who, of their own free-will and choice, abide in the midst of collected Africans, often have their infants nursed from the breasts of African women, grow up in the companionship of African playmates, pass their early and their later years perpetually leaning on African attendants, are perpetually tempted, and not seldom effectually tempted, to indulge in African recreations; supported in affluence on the proceeds of African labor, from youth to age perpetually familiar with the tones of African voices, and conversant with the workings of African minds, and exalted to what

6

themselves suppose and esteem to be the highest pinnacles of social and political eminence, by nothing but the upholding of African subordinates, — to be, to do, and to suffer all this from generation to generation, and come off at the end uncontaminated with any considerable traits of African character, is simply impossible. "Evil communications corrupt good manners." Two individuals of different grades of moral elevation and improvement can hardly be brought in contact, to any considerable extent, without each participating, to some extent, in the character of the other. Two masses of population, of different grades of civilization, *can never* be continuously interspersed, as are the whites and blacks in one of the Slave States, and avoid the efficient action of that natural law which tends to bring both to a common, medium level. The more degraded will be elevated; the more elevated will be brought down.

Many traits of character which have been thus imparted to the white from the colored race, by long and familiar intercommunication in the Slave States, it would be invidious to specify. But one of these, if possible, more prominent and more important than any other, it is necessary here to consider. That trait is AFRICAN DESPOTISM, — unmitigated by any of the amenities of revealed religion, or of modern learning or civilization, imported in the form of masses of the vilest barbarians, and participated in through the medium of a willing, constant, intimate, and lifelong intercommunication by the white race in Slave States.

This, as all other forms of despotism, necessarily exists in two divisions, — in the imperious usurpation of dictatorial power on the part of a few over the many, and in the cringing acquiescence under this dictation, on the part of the many. One of these divisions cannot long exist without the other; and the one is necessarily produced and propagated by the presence of the other. The former, or usurping, dictatorial class were not imported from Africa. These were generated on the spot by the presence of the servile masses. Yet the rights and authority in which they flourish were imported, and are purely African. A barbarous father sold his child to the brutal slave-trader; a bloody chief of an abject tribe surprised a sleeping village, and, after murdering a portion of its inhabitants, sold the rest to the slave-trader for rum and tobacco. Titles thus acquired to the lifelong services of the remotest descendants of these abject, godless captives, are transferred to an American master, and in these he flourishes; with the effect, it is true, to better the condition of the slave, for it does not admit of being made worse; but with the effect on himself, to deprive him of all ability and disposition to act an honest part as a citizen of a democratic community, in supporting the principles and institutions of popular self-government, or to understand that, looking at the matter with any other than the eyes of an African despot, it is not only undemocratic, but unutterably mean, cruel, unjust, and dishonorable, to recognize any such title as that by which the negro is held in bondage, or to fatten in useless idleness on the unrequited toil of a slave, compelled to labor by the force of superior intelligence and combination.

The presence of these abject masses of Africans, by elevating their owners into the position of lords and nobles, and by depriving the non-slave-holding whites, to a great extent, of the usual opportunities of productive labor, and also by rendering labor of the whites disreputable, thereby confining down the non-slave-holding whites, for the most part, to a state of hopeless poverty and idleness, perfected what the presence of nobles and great men had early begun, — the separation of Southern society into the two monarchical grades of high and influential few, and low and uninfluential many; thus sealing and rendering perpetual a social state inimical to democracy.

The blacks, not only by the force of their example, remaining in contented ignorance, but by spreading out the white population so sparsely as to render public free schools ill-convenient for children to attend, contributed much to prevent that degree of general intelligence among the whites, without which affairs of government cannot safely be intrusted to the hands of the public at large.

6*

XI.

THE last chapter was to have completed our
notice of the causes that acted in the Southern
States to stop the progress of those sentiments
of freedom which had cleared the North of
slaves. The closing passages of that chapter
verged upon what is the stated aim of this,
namely, to notice the effects of slavery while it
was retained, to counteract the growth and to
turn back the progress of the principles of free
government. The influence exerted on the
white community by that heathen mass, so distributed as to come in contact with them at
almost every point, cannot be overestimated in
its effect of imparting to American minds African opinions and sentiments of what is advantageous, what is proper, and what is right, in
regard to ownership, by one man, of property in
the life and services, the bone, muscle, and brain,
of another. The whole tone and spirit of the

Anglo-Saxon mind and character must have been degraded and demoralized by the contaminating influence of heathen associates — must have become essentially Africanized — before this doctrine of property in man could have been permanently introduced.

But, having been once introduced, approved of, and rendered permanent, it requires but a glance to show that the deepest, darkest, form of despotism had been planted there, so that wherever African slavery existed, and was permanently preferred to a state of society where all are free, there this lowest form of heathen despotism obtained in principle and in practice, and slavery and despotism mutually confirmed each other, and both necessarily increased and extended, till they reached and confronted the vital forces of a sincere democracy, there to rage and rave and perish, as they are now doing in the existing war.

Much of American slave-holding is to be attributed to accident, and not to design or choice. In such cases, principles of free government were held and cherished sincerely, and without being greatly counteracted by the unwilling, accidental, holding of the relation of master. Such was the case of Washington himself, of Jefferson, of Clay, and doubtless of the vast majority of slave-owners in the latter colonial times, and in the early history of the States. They lacked only opportunity, a sense of the important influence slavery was secretly exerting against free government, and a more energetic enforcement of their own hearty preference in respect to it, to have freed themselves from its contaminating power. These, however, they lacked. They sluggishly acquiesced in its continuance. The degenerating, degrading influence of African associations acted on their descendants more and more in each succeeding generation, until the love and approbation of ownership in slaves began generally to prevail, and with it all real attachment to the principles and institutions of free government were silently and unconsciously, but effectually and thoroughly, undermined and uprooted; and every one became unwittingly prepared to take his place at a greater or less elevation in the common grading of subordinates beneath a despotic head.

I say *every one* became unwittingly thus prepared; for if there had been one uncontaminated freeman left, he would have pronounced himself by severing that despotic head from the shoulders on which it was sustained, ere the meshes of tyrannical control had been woven around him, and his bleeding land laid desolate merely

to save that head from being severed. Perhaps this remark should be modified in favor
of some whom compulsory distance or prison
walls prevent from performing the desire of
their hearts.

XII.

FROM the influence of climate, rendering the negroes prolific and content, and the whites averse to industry and toil; from the influence of a soil so rich as to allow the thriftless system to continue; from the influence of the numbers of slaves, rendering emancipation difficult and hazardous; from the social influence of the blacks, acting to depress and Africanize the civilization of the whites, and to import and impart the property-title, and the type-African, which is the lowest form of despotism; and from the influence of the numbers of the blacks in spreading the white population so sparsely that free schools could not be maintained; and perhaps from the influence of still other causes which have been overlooked, — it came to pass that the progress of the principles of free government, which had abolished slavery in the Northern States, was stayed at Mason & Dixon's line. Slavery remained, and still remains, un-

70

abolished, and, till recently, prospering in the Southern States. What lies before us now is to observe in detail the several ways in which this existing institution necessarily acts to convert back to the principles of political despotism the people of those Southern States who had once given in, with some emphasis, their adherence to the principles and (as far as white persons are concerned) to the practices of civil freedom.

And, first, we are reminded by the language in which the above proposition is necessarily stated, that there is, and must be, a radical incongruity, a deep, internal self-contradiction in the pretence of adopting or adhering to the principles of free government for one class of persons, while the same franchise is totally denied to another class in the same community, — the broadest, free government for whites, and the deepest, darkest despotism for blacks in the same community, and on the same soil.

To obviate the bad appearance and bad result of this unhappy combination of despotism and democracy in the South, it is to be remembered, as already remarked, that much of the slave-holding, as in the case of Washington and his compeers, was accidental and without any sincere participation in the governmental principle which willing and persistent slave-holding in-volves.*

How far the practice of slave-holding, where the principle is rejected, will act gradually and silently to corrupt and undermine opinions and preferences favorable to free government, is a question that we cannot definitely decide. Where the unwilling slave-holder is constantly occupied, as were the fathers of the Republic, in elaborating the form, and erecting the institutions, of free government, the presence of this odious hulk of despotism would, doubtless, provoke a spirit of reaction against the governmental principle on which it is based. But, where the actual slave-owner, though favorable to free government, is left unoccupied by any employment that puts his love of freedom in active and trying exercise, although that love of freedom may not be consciously or entirely subverted by the practice of slave-holding, yet it will not be strange if his continual practical acquiescence in a system which he disapproves should have the effect to blunt his apprehension of what freedom really consists in, and so to

* Those readers who are disposed to pursue a definite and extended inquiry into the expressed views of the fathers and founders of this government, on the subject of "negroes as slaves, as citizens, and as soldiers," will find the material for such investigation collected ready to their hand, in *An Historical Research*, by George Livermore. Boston: A. Williams & Company, 1863.

accustom him to submit to doing what he disapproves that he would at length be found to be the fit man to enlist under the rankest despot, to fight for the " LIBERTY " of *holding other men in bondage*. But there is still a very wide difference between the willing and persistent, and the accidental and unwilling, holding of slaves, in respect to the influence which slave-holding exerts to undemocratize the master.

Besides the accidental and unwilling character of much of the slave-holding that has characterized the South, one other condition has intervened essentially to modify the influence which slave-holding would otherwise exert to counteract the perfecting and the spread of principles of civil freedom. It is the unfitness of the negro, by reason of ignorance and vice, and of his low, spiritless, and barbarian traits, either to be himself profited by possessing the franchises of freemen, or to be a safe or useful member of a democratic community.

There is no denying that negroes when freshly imported from their barbarous African homes, — where, according to the best of testimony, " nine-tenths of the inhabitants are slaves to the other tenth," — are utterly unfit to be intrusted with the privileges of free citizenship in an enlight-

17

ened community.   And, during this pupilage of degraded feebleness and ignorance, which, where large masses of them are together, may last for generations, it is hardly violating the principles of civil freedom, to hold them dependent on masters as their proper guardians.   This it was that rendered slavery in colonial and Revolutionary times, compatible with the inception, growth, and all-conquering progress of the principles of civil freedom.   And this, together with the large amount of unwilling slave-holding that existed at the time the Constitution was adopted, rendered the authors and adopters of that instrument so little concerned about the anti-republican tendencies of the institution which they neglected to extirpate.

XIII.

HISTORICAL events of the highest magnitude and importance often fail to be appreciated, because they take place gradually. Such was the case in the transition of negro slavery, by which it passed from the mild, accidental form, which marked the first century or more of its existence in this country, to the positiveness and virulence of its character in later years. Had the boundaries of the original colonies remained unchanged, had the early character of our commercial exports not altered, and the political arena been free from agitation on the subject of slavery, then might the action of the institution, in respect to its influence on our peculiar civil system, have remained harmless as at first. But, unfortunately, neither of these conditions of its harmlessness was preserved. Our Western boundaries were extended until they embraced additional territory enough for a magnificent empire, of the richest of soils, and under the same Southern sun. This gave to slaves a value that they never possessed in colonial times, and added new rivets to the bondage that previously appeared almost ready to fall off of its own accord. Next came, gradually, the discoveries, that cotton was one of the most desirable textile staples in the world, that every human being wanted it, in no stinted supply, for clothing, and could afford to pay well, according to his means, rather than be deprived of its use, that the soil and climate of the Southern States, with this newly-acquired Southern territory, were best adapted of any known to the production of this desired staple, and that slave-labor was better adapted to its cultivation than to any other known branch of industry. Next came the improvements in machinery for the cleaning and manufacture of cotton, which increased the demand for it ten thousand fold. The market money-value of negro slaves rose five hundred per cent., and settled forever, on the wrong side, the question whether the spreading application of the principles of free government should peaceably progress any farther in opposition to the sway of this darkest form of African despotism.

Now was the time, as soon as the above facts

became developed, to have recognized a state of irreconcilable war between slave-holders and their adherents on the one hand, and the upholders of the principles on which the civil institutions of our country had been founded, on the other hand. But the inherent imbecility of popular governments, as compared with monarchies, in respect to matters of war and self-defence; the cupidity of those at the North who contrived to share in the profits of lucrative slave-holding, and the intrigue of the slave-holders to keep everything quiet until they could corrupt the Northern people, and grasp the reins of power in the general government, all wrought together to prevent alarm, until the designs of despotism had progressed so far that, in the estimation of disinterested European statesmen and observers, the fate of free governments in general, and of the United States in particular, was sealed, before the people of the Northern States allowed themselves to believe that anything was seriously amiss with them.

While the area of fertile Southern territory was being extended, and the enormous and lucrative business of cotton production was being developed, and the pecuniary value of slaves was being doubled over and over again, thus fixing them in their state of bondage beyond the

7*

hope of any *peaceable* release or relaxation, another change was silently and gradually taking
place, which enhanced the tyrannical and op-
pressive nature of their bondage, about in the
same proportion in which its perpetuity became
inevitable. This was, the growing intelligence,
civilization, and Christian enlightenment, of the
negroes, which fitted them daily more and more
to enjoy the privileges, and to discharge the
duties, of freemen ; thereby rendering it daily a
greater and greater outrage on the principles
of free government to hold them in servitude.

We have before remarked that where two
masses of population, of different degrees of
elevation and enlightenment, were thrown together on terms of intimate and constant interchange, the result must be, not only that the
more elevated would be brought down, but the
more degraded would be elevated, until a common
medium level should have been reached by each.
The master may designedly and systematically
withhold from his slave the art of reading, and
all instruction tending to his enlightenment and
elevation ; but it is not within the power of that
master to prevent the slave from learning a
lesson for his improvement every time he looks
on, or listens to, a person more intelligent, more
civilized, or more a Christian, than himself. This

course of improvement must go on, on the part
of the blacks, until their masters, and those
whites with whom they come in contact, in their
downward course, come to a level where the
two grades of civilization meet, and the negro
has no more of civilization, manhood, or Christianity, to learn of his once superior master. In
proportion as the negro thus becomes elevated,
intelligent, and fit for freedom, the policy and
the practice that confine him down to servitude become bereft of palliation, and stand
out in active and confessed hostility to the
principles of all free government.

XIV.

THE ULTIMATE, POSITIVE, AND EFFICIENT, ACTION OF SLAVE-
HOLDING IN RADICALLY CONVERTING THE SENTIMENTS OF
THE SOUTHERN PEOPLE BACK FROM DEMOCRACY TO DES-
POTISM.

SERIOUS and important occupation has a powerful influence in moulding the sentiments of
one who is heartily occupied therein. The trying labors and sacrifices of the Revolutionary
struggle, with the discussions which preceded
and followed them, acted strongly to generate
and confirm a love of freedom in the hearts
of those, on the American side, by whom these
toils and sacrifices were sustained. The period which we are now about to consider is
one in which such occupations and their influence have long since passed away. The
enervating, corrupting, influences of protracted peace and unexampled affluence have succeeded to the struggles and hardships of Revolutionary and colonial times. The pursuit of
personal aggrandizement has succeeded to an
absorbing interest in the nation's welfare. In
those States where slavery never extensively

existed, and has been abolished, agriculture, mechanics, and every industrial pursuit, are followed with an earnestness and success unparalleled under monarchical government.

In those States where slavery still flourishes, supine submissiveness to ignorance and poverty and the domination of the few, seizes on the many; while the possession and management of acres and of slaves, and the influence and emoluments of public office, form the objects of successful aspiration to the few, — the " master race," as some of their public orators have the modesty to call themselves.

The palliation of slavery, that grew out of the unfitness of the negroes for freedom, has largely passed away. The comparative indifference with which slave-owners formerly regarded their right of property in the slave, owing to their small pecuniary value, and to the ugly incongruity between the master's claims for freedom for himself, and for secure bondage for his negro, has also passed away. His African associations have implanted in the mind of the master an opinion favorable to the justice and propriety of his claim on the services of his slave. The increased numbers of his fellow-slave-holders, and the increased age of the institution, confirm the same opinion, and quiet feelings of uneasiness respecting the incongruity of his claims. The enlarged bounds of fertile slave territory dispel apprehensions of trouble from the impoverishment of the soil; and the lucrativeness of cotton-raising insures him large pecuniary returns, either for raising cotton or for raising slaves. Now what a school is this in which to learn democracy, and perfect these preferences for popular freedom which are not mature!* At the same time and in the same proportion in which negroes have become more fitted to be free, and their labor has become more valuable, arose the necessity for guarding against insurrection, and for systematic legislation and police regulations, rendering this kind of property secure. Laws had to be passed by each State, prohibiting the instruction of slaves, lest their learning should render them more desirous of freedom, more competent to secure it, and more accessible to the approaches of de-

---

* The term republic, though sometimes used as substantially synonymous with democracy, may with propriety be applied to a republic of slave-holders, or a leagued band of aristocrats. So far as the latter is its true import, the Constitution of the United States, in its provision that the government of each several State shall be republican, simply covers up the seeds of its own destruction. So far as the import of the word is synonymous with democracy, this provision of the general Constitution has been violated every time a Slave State has been admitted to the Union. Democracy and Despotism divide the universe of civil affairs between them. There is and can be no middle ground that will not, of necessity, soon merge itself in the one or the other.

signing disturbers of the patriarchal system. Also, laws by each State prohibiting emancipation within its bounds, and the ingress of free negroes ; lest individual owners, who felt averse to slave-trading, should free vicious negroes, to save themselves the most unpleasant task of controlling them, and the number and character of the free colored population should thereby become such as to make slaves uneasy, and endanger the public safety. Thus slave-holding became more and more consolidated into a system, and the individual owner became less and less at liberty to pursue any course 'which was not dictated by regard for the interests and quiet of all slave-holders.

The effect of this consolidation — the imposed necessity of acting together for the protection of an imperilled interest — was not only a great advance toward monarchy ; itself constitutes a great essential element of monarchy.

It was the necessity of defending national existence amidst menacing or actually hostile nations that first induced the prevalence of monarchy. Produce one great, all-absorbing interest of a class, or section, even in a republic, and let it be surrounded by sentiments and interests adverse to its prosperity, and you have got a consolidation of peculiar interests. You will

soon have, on the part of their holders, a unanimity of views and a willing acquiescence in
anything which promises to subserve and render
those peculiar and imperilled interests secure.
You have got seven-tenths of all that is requisite to a monarchy, and the other three-tenths
cannot, from the nature of things, be long wanting. It was this unanimity, resulting from necessary consolidation on this peculiar interest, that
gave to some 60,000 Southern slave-holders a
perpetually preponderating influence in the affairs of the general government, which neither
one nor all of the varying political interests, and
combinations of half as many millions of other
population have been able to countervail.

Combinations on an imperilled interest like
this, are necessarily fatal to any republic, not
itself entirely comprehended in the combination.

Had the stakes involved in the preservation
of slavery been of less pecuniary value, or had
the principles and practices of slavery been less
repugnant to everything around them, then
had the consolidation been less constraining, and
the results less decisive. Had the interests of
slave-holders remained unimportant as at the
time of the Revolution, then had they remained
as harmless. But the unexpected and unex-

ampled rise of the importance of slave-holders' interests, taking place contemporaneously with the spread and maturing of the principles and forms of free government, developed the latent antagonism of the two systems, and necessitated the present war, which might have been calculated years ago, by any skilful and clear-minded statesman, with as much certainty as the astronomer calculates an eclipse.

8

XV.

BESIDES obtaining a just apprehension of the influence of slavery in general, to counteract the progress of free government, we are here to examine the influence in this direction of African slavery as it exists in this country, and also as it has existed during recent years, in contradistinction from the same as it existed at and before the founding of our free institutions. The question obtrudes itself for answer, Why has the institution which at, and prior to, the adoption of the Constitution exerted little or no influence adverse to the rise and establishment of civil freedom, since exerted so powerful an influence as to convert back again to principles of the darkest despotism the sons of sires who, amidst the acting of the same slavery system, suffered and bled for freedom? The answer is to be found in the altered action of the system. At the same time that slaves and their labor have risen enormously

in money value, and a stringent and powerful
police system has had to be everywhere put in
operation for the security of this peculiar species
of property, the slaves themselves, having advanced greatly in attaining the language, sentiments, intelligence, and civilization of their masters, feel more and more keenly the wrong that
is done them by the system, and react against it
with more pressing and perpetual elasticity.

The fact that no arguments are heard from
their lips against the policy of their enslavement,
that few fights are made by them to demonstrate
their unwillingness to remain longer enslaved,
that only now and then a plot is discovered for
a general rising to free themselves, does not
prove that there is no strong and ceaseless pressure on their part against the confines that cir-
cumscribe their freedom ; they rather prove the
success with which their masters have learned
the arts that despots use to keep their victims in
subjugation.   It is not our object here to discuss
the right or wrong of slavery.   That there is
such a distinction, and that it is important to be
attended to, we freely admit ; but that is not the
theme of these remarks.   These pages are not
intended to contain an essay on morals or religion ; they profess to deal with politics purely ;
and with these only in reference to despotism
and democracy, and the relations or repulsions

that necessarily exist between them. Of this subject we treat, as it applies to, and is illustrated by, the past history and present condition of affairs in the United States,— the home and seat of the only permanent democratic government the history of the world has yet presented. Therefore, when we speak of the stringent legislation and police arrangements that have been gradually built up around the slaves to keep them safe, at the same time and in the same proportion in which the money-value of these slaves has gradually and enormously increased; and while we speak of the gradually increasing fitness of the slaves for freedom, and their consequently increasing desire and demand for freedom, which takes place at the same time that the provisions for keeping them securely in bondage are tightened and strengthened, our object is not to direct attention to the moral crime of slavery at all, but purely to present the fact of the perpetually increasing intensity of the conflict between slavery and freedom, between despotism and democracy, — the development of the latent and necessary conflict on the part of the negroes to be free, and on the part of the masters to retain them in secure and profitable subservience to their lust of power and of gain. Our object in turning attention to the constantly increasing intensity of this conflict is not to show the cruelty or the moral wrong of keeping the negroes still in servitude, but to point out the tremendous and necessary effect of the perpetually intensifying strife to mature and perfect those masters, and such as are acting with them, in the spirit and the precepts, the principles and practices, of despotism,—of exercising despotic and dictatorial control over their fellow-men.

Among the smaller changes that have taken place, which have contributed to make up the whole great sum of altered circumstances which give to slavery, as it recently existed, an hundred-fold the power it once possessed to despotize American democracy, is that mutual exchange by which not only has the African imparted to his American master much of his barbaric character, and especially his native leanings toward the darkest form of despotism, but in return has received not only gradual enlightenment, civilization, and Christianity, but also a preference and fitness for the institutions of free government. The history of the freed slaves colonized in Liberia demonstrates this. And the possessing of this predisposition for free government, which they could have acquired nowhere but in this country, makes their bondage more grievous to them, and their reaction against imposed restraints more incessant and intense.

8*

XVI.

WE now propose to examine more in detail the practical workings of those principles, and that, too, under the circumstances which we have above stated and defined.

The negroes have now come to be three or four millions. The price of a field-hand has risen from its former range of from one to three hundred dollars to cotton-planting value of from ten to fifteen hundred dollars, and a ready cash sale at that. What is the mode of operating to render this amount of property secure and productive?

The whole power of the United States army and navy is understood to stand pledged to suppress insurrection and to return fugitive slaves.

There is then some danger that large or small portions of this valuable property shall make use of its legs and run away. There is also danger, — grave enough, in the incipient stage

90

in which the peril existed seventy-five years ago, to deserve a constitutional provision, — that this intelligent property, of which "its follies and its crimes have stamped it man," should take to itself the weapons of vengeance and inflict immense sufferings on those whom it supposes to be the authors of its conscious wrongs.

This danger is no less than the danger of losing an aggregate of twenty-six hundred millions of dollars' worth of property, and of the devastation of a greater or less portion of the soil of the Southern States, with the slaughter of its white inhabitants. These surely are grave perils, and the weight of them is sufficient of itself to make despots of as many men as are left to feel that the responsibility of providing against these perils rests upon themselves.

The strain and pressure of such a responsibility is probably entirely beyond the comprehension of one who has been born and educated in the confiding quiet and equal privileges of democratic civilization. Such an one has no experience in his history in which to find a simile that would parallel for an hour the strain of this life-long responsibility that rests more or less sensibly on every intelligent and habitual dweller in a slave-holding community, but more sensibly and immediately on the slave-holder himself who has a wife and children, parents, brothers, sisters, and friends, involved with him in the same more or less imminent peril. One, from prodigality or moral refinement. may divest himself of any desire or esteem for the pecuniary value represented by property which statutes of the country recognize and guarantee in slaves; but the terrible consequences of permitting or provoking any extensive struggle on their part to free themselves must appall the stoutest heart that is not prepared to sport with wide-spread devastation and human suffering and slaughter.

With this standing peril ever hanging over them. it may at first be supposed, that the Southern mind had become callous to its force; but history, and somewhat extended personal observation, have convinced the author that, from the passion-kindling influence of the climate, from the absence of other things to displace this from the attention, or from other causes, the fear of slave insurrection, instead of being deadened by use, remains extremely vivid, if it does not grow increasingly so, in the majority of Southern minds. I knew the ladies of an extensive neighborhood, in a Slave State, with scarcely any exception, to pass a week of sleepless anxiety and fear, because they heard a rumor that some barges filled with negroes were seen to pass a neighboring river.

Accustomed from infancy to revel in the broadest liberty that ever was coupled with the sweets of civilization, comparatively few men in the Northern States are acquainted with any object of fear, in heaven, earth, or hell, that is capable of imposing on them the practical restraint which the slave-holder, and those connected with him, ordinarily feel, from the fear of a slave insurrection.* It is an imposed restraint which they never question, never parley with. Its dominion over them is absolute. And one of the functions of this absolute allegiance is, never to allow its authority to be questioned by others, within their borders or without them, so far as they have the power to prevent.

His Creator — and it is rare to find a Southern man who questions either his existence or his claims — may or may not be obeyed. That is a matter which every individual is perfectly free to exercise his own preference upon. The au-

---

* The tens of thousands of lives, and the hundreds of millions of money, which the existing war is yearly extorting from the Northern people, has roused in few if any of the minds of the millions who remain at home, the amount of serious earnestness and persistent devotion which instantly took possession of the mind of each intelligent Southerner, tho moment he was called to contemplate a serious disturbance of the power-imposed quiet of their slaves.

thority of the country's laws and government, every one is usually considered at liberty to regard or disregard as he pleases. So also with the claims of truth, justice, and humanity. But any risk of raising a slave insurrection is not to be incurred, come what will.

What is a republic, what is a democracy, under such circumstances? What, but a conventional equality of command in a community of despots?

Twenty-six senators, and three or four times that number of representatives from the Southern States, assemble annually at the national capitol, professedly to legislate for the benefit of the common population of the whole country, and under oath to support the common government; but, in reality, a leagued band, trained and disciplined under recognized leaders, armed with side-arms of the carnal sort, and with all the panoply of rhetoric, logic, sophistry, parliamentary tactics, diplomatic guile, political effrontery, and county-court tergiversation. But what are they there to do? One thing, — the same that they have done from infancy, and will continue to do as long as breath is in them and they have the power of voluntary motion, — the thing which will be done effectually in those legislative halls and elsewhere, wherever these

men are found, their own oaths, and the learning, the logic, the rights, and the numbers of
their opponents to the contrary notwithstanding,
viz : see to it that the absolute and practically
unlimited despotic power of masters over their
slaves remains undisturbed, unapproached by
any unfriendly restriction, check, or limitation ;
see that no law is passed, and no act unrebuked,
unrevenged, is performed, that would in the
remotest manner encourage a slave to run away
from his master, or inspire in the negroes, as a
class, the faintest gleam of hope or expectation
that their oppressed condition is to be ameliorat-
ed.   In other words, the one unvarying task of
those assembled legislators from the Southern
States — the thing which they will be perfectly
sure to see accomplished at all times and in all
places, and despite all difficulties and opposition
— is to provide that the dominion of that malign
divinity, the presiding genius of slave-holding,
the very soul and essence of the darkest, deepest, and most damning, form of despotism, before
whom they have bowed down and worshipped
all their lives, and (though less devoutly) their
fathers before them, remains unmolested, unin-
fringed upon.   This worship they pay and this
service they perform, not more because they
love to than because they must.   To escape the

inexorable exigency of the position in which they have been born, requires a breadth of comprehension, ability, and benevolence, which probably it is not possible should be generated in the walks of slave-holders.

XVII.

INTENSITY OF THE ANTAGONISM BETWEEN THE PRINCIPLES OF FREE GOVERNMENT AND THE PRINCIPLES ON WHICH SLAVES ARE GOVERNED — THE LATTER ANALYZED — THE PRECEPT — THE PENALTY — CHECKS ON THE LATTER.

WHY have the upbuildings and outgrowths of institutions of benevolence, philanthropy, religion, and missionary zeal, which have preëminently characterized, adorned, and blessed, our common land, giving the powerful weight of their testimony in favor of the beneficent influence of free government, been able to accomplish so little in mitigating the severe exactions made upon the Southern slave, — in softening the sharp iron of the despotism which has this prone servitude for its base ?

The answer is found in the same facts that account for the turning back of the wave of free principles, which, sweeping from the North, extinguished slavery in one-half of the original States.

The opportunity to peaceably abolish slavery from the Southern States presented itself at the time of the adoption of the present form of our general government. But it was an opportunity that soon passed, to return no more. The latent antagonism that existed between the principles of despotism and democracy became rapidly developed by the constantly irritating contact of the two, and it soon became impossible to modify either, until the one should be extinguished utterly by the armed and bloody triumph of the other. As well might one go on a mission of peace to the eternal abode of devils and damned spirits, expecting to harmonize their jarring strifes, and to produce an enduring compromise between the conflicting passions of those who there abide, as think effectually to obviate or compromise the conflict that has raged in this country for the last half-century, for the most part with unbloody weapons, but which has now assumed the more natural and effective form of fierce and bloody, not to say exterminating, war. Any truce, or compromise, or compact, or division of territory, that could be agreed upon, would' of necessity be only the inauguration of interminable, vexatious, bloody, and disastrous, hostilities.

Look at the mode of operation by which murmurs are quieted, and aspirations after freedom suppressed, by masters among their slaves. In doing this, we may as well start with the practice at its origin, in Africa, where "nine-tenths of the population are slaves to the other tenth," * where the lives of slaves are held at so cheap a rate, that they are slaughtered by hundreds, as a token of respect to a deceased monarch. There, we need not be told, that physical sufferings, unto permanent maiming, and the death penalty, are inflicted without stint, wherever and whenever the owner of a slave supposes he has any occasion to inflict them. In the hands of the slave-trader who brings them across the ocean, or buys them to sell again after they arrive, the same mode of government prevails, mitigated by nothing but the increased pecuniary value of the slave, and the corresponding pecuniary loss, in case of crippling or killing him, as he approaches the plantation where he is to spend his life of labor.

When arrived on that plantation, and fixed in his condition for life, and for the lives of his posterity after him, the precept by which he is, and is to be, governed is still the will and pleasure of his owner, and the penalty of violating that precept is physical suffering, restrained only by the pecuniary estimation in which he is held,

* This statement is quoted verbally from Commodore Gregory, of the U. S. Navy, who spent ten years in service on the African coast.

the greater or less humanity of his master, and perhaps a law of the State, prescribing some punishment for killing him, provided the murder is confessedly unprovoked, and can be proved by the testimony of white witnesses.

Look at these three items, that alone tend to mitigate the intensity of Africa's barbarous despotism.

The high pecuniary value at which the slave is held by his master acts to guard that slave from the extreme of inhuman punishment and death. Does this avail anything to obviate the extreme degradation of his servile condition, or the despotic supremacy of his master over him? If it does, then let us make due allowance. But though the degradation of the slave whose master values him at a high price appears not in every sense to be as low as that of one whose life would be sacrificed for a trifle, yet the negro, in his more valuable estate, is probably the more intelligent, feels this servitude more, and, though his elevation changes the field of its operation, it does not, probably, mitigate the tyrannous intent and purpose of his master in holding him in bondage. Indeed, the intention of the master, in holding the high-priced, intelligent negro in a bondage which he strongly resists, is probably more tyrannical than that which holds the low-priced slave, who scarcely has the intelligence or the manhood to desire to be free. And what we are looking for, in this investigation, is not the degradation or suffering of the slave, or anything else, other than the despotic principle, and purpose, and action, of the master; and this, too, only as the *exercise* of this despotic principle, or purpose, on the part of the master, tends to confirm itself, and to make him radically a despot.

The legal restriction in the Slave States, against the master taking the life of his slave, is just enough to constitute a legislative acknowledgment that the negroes are human beings, without practical force enough to afford them any substantial protection, even of their lives. The legal requirement in respect to testimony is so easily evaded, and the assertion of resistance, or assault, on the part of the negro, is so easily maintained by the master, that conviction for the murder of a slave, if the murder had been conducted with any prudent safeguard against notoriety, would be impossible. But the operation of pecuniary interest which the master has in his slave constitutes quite an ample protection in this regard.

9*

XVIII.

THE enlightened benevolence of the American master — although this is a very uncertain
quantity, yet, in the aggregate, in comparison
with the murderous cruelty of the African master, it is exceedingly great and precious — constitutes the chief cause of mitigating the exercise
of that tyrannical authority which the American
slave-owner possesses; thereby mitigating the
reactive effect which the exercise of that authority would have, to annihilate the remnant of his
own free principles. The enjoyment of ease
and affluence tends to make one generous
toward others. The Africanization which the
master's mind has undergone, through the influence of negro educating and negro society, has
not entirely reversed this tendency.

If the principles of free government still retain any sway in the master's mind, they will
join their influence to that of a native or acquired

benevolence, inducing that master to leave unused much of the despotic power over his slave,
with which the civil code of his State invests
him. Hence arose that softening-down of the
claims and pretensions of mastership which had
well-nigh yielded up the whole system of slavery,
at about the period of the adoption of the
Federal Constitution. Hence, also, that lack of
sympathy with the slave system, which caused it
to be absolutely abhorred by thousands who
continued to practice it from the force of circumstances, which they lacked the skill and energy
to control.

But all of these mitigating influences were
doomed to meet their limit, and their final defeat
and reversal, in the State necessity, as it may be
called, — the necessity of treating the negroes
in such a way as would secure the public welfare,
beyond a peradventure, against insurrectionary
disturbance. What this mode of treatment is,
it is not left wholly to individual judgment to
decide. Education, universal usage, and an
exacting public sentiment, determine that it
shall be such usage as will effectually keep down
all manifest aspirations after a better condition,
— that the art of reading and writing, and all
means of increased intelligence shall be, as far
as possible, inhibited, — that the personal property

held by slaves shall be kept down as near as possible to zero ; especially the possession of anything that might be used as an offensive or defensive weapon shall not be permitted; that the orders of the master, any member of his white family, or his overseer, shall be performed, right or wrong, under penalty of the severest chastisement. After all this has been exacted and complied with, I know not that it is adding anything, to say that the most obsequious deference is exacted of, and paid by, every negro, to every white person of the master-class when in his presence.

The justice of the master's claim to everything the negro is, or has, or can produce, is never permitted for a moment to be questioned. The negro has no rights, is to advance none, to defend none. Food and clothing of some sort, and attendance when sick, are secured to him by the master's property interest in his health and efficiency. Other than these, it is deemed to be extremely imprudent to allow a negro to claim as his any right or privilege whatever. To do so would open the way for negroes to make larger and larger claims, and would certainly lead to some struggle on their part to maintain and enforce such claims. The only way to keep them quiet is not to allow them to claim as their right anything whatever, or to possess anything but what their master pleases graciously to allow. Here is the limit that is set to the exercise of benevolence or free principles on the part of the master among his negroes. The exigencies of the public safety forbid these bounds to be enlarged, and enforce this prohibition by the peril of all the untold loss and horrors of servile insurrection.

Look for a moment at the means by which the slave-owner, be he benevolent or malevolent, be he monarchist or republican, *must* enforce upon his negro this abnegation of *all* claims to any personal right, — this implicit, unquestioning obedience to his owner's will. Suppose a negro slave to question or resist his master's right to dispose of him as he pleases. It matters not when, or where, or in what manner, this lack of submissiveness is manifested. There is one law for that refractory slave, and, like the laws of the Medes and Persians, it changes not. Physical suffering must be meted out till that rebellious will is broken. The punishment may be administered by the owner in person, or by his deputy. The master may or may not superintend and prescribe the limit. The punishment must emanate from the master's right, and is to vindicate and sustain his authority, and it is not optional with that master whether to punish or not. The first condition of owning a slave, according to the African system Americanized, the system universally practised in the Southern States, is to enforce submission by corporal punishment to any needed extent; and every negro and every intelligent white person in the South knows this to be so. So that to own a slave and not whip him, is as impossible as it is to live in the body without breathing, except so far as the slave anticipates the whipping, and prevents it by sincere, unvarying, submissive obedience. Other than this, there is no alternative, except to sell the slave, — a punishment which he usually dreads next to death.

This whipping is not often done in public. It is not usually done in the presence of the white family, or where they will even hear the negro's cries. The generally prevailing opinion among masters is, that the less of it is done, the better; and the more silently, the better. That every expedient of successful government should be resorted to in order to avoid it, both on account of its unpleasantness, its brutifying effect on the master, or those who act under him, and the danger of damage to the slave. But, however

obscurely concealed, however remotely postponed, there it is, known, calculated on, and
inevitable; the slave that refuses to submit
implicitly to his master must be whipped till he
yields.

XIX.

WE have, then, from an analysis of slavery, this result: The slave is deprived of *all* rights, has all aspirations after liberty suppressed, is reduced to, and retained in, implicit subjection to his master's will. He is placed in this position by statute laws recognizing the claim of an African captor, or purchaser, to the lifelong services of his slave, and of that slave's descendants, and also recognizing this claim, now termed a right, as it stands transferred from an African to an American owner. This law is enforced, and the benefits of this right are exacted, by the ever-present fact or fear of corporal suffering, inflicted to an unlimited extent by the authority, and according to the will, of the slave-owner. Any mitigation of these conditions is accidental, —is due to the kindness and the skill, the benevolent and freedom-loving spirit which the master may happen to possess; and is limited and restrained by the imminent danger that public disturbance and incalculable calamity will result

108

from any considerable relaxation, or failure to enforce his claim, on the part of the master.

Now, and here, the very important question arises, How long can a man occupy, exercise, and enforce the claims of a master on his slaves, without becoming himself imbued with the spirit and principles of a despot, and without having his attachment to the principles of free government sadly undermined ?

Certainly, if that man has in his composition the average natural amount of logic, he must exercise the functions of master with extreme reluctance, and must find his most cherished and indulged associates remote from the servility of slaves, or, before he is aware of it, the principles of free government, as held by him, will have become a mere inoperative, dreamlike theory, however strongly he may suppose himself to be attached to them ; and the whole tendency and habit of his mind and character will have been moulded to every lineament of a despot.

While the slave system was in its incipiency, while the master held the unenlightened African as much from motives of benevolence as of gain, and cared little whether the worthless wretches were retained or free, slave-holding could not have had much power to mould the principles and political habits of the master.   But, as the

10

established institutions of the country began to exert a pressure on that master in favor of the principles of free government, and to demand from him a sincere and active support; as the negro became more and more enlightened and fit for freedom, and more and more desirous of obtaining it, thus exerting a constantly increasing pressure against the force that kept him down in servitude; and as, at the same time, the high and advancing price of slave-labor induced the slave-holder, from motives of pecuniary gain, to grasp with new vigor, and exercise with new stringency, the power by which he held his slave in bondage, — then it was that the power of the practice of slave-holding became irresistible to mould the governmental principles of the slave-holder; then it was that the whole Southern mind became so tempered with, and infected by, the intoxicating sweets of despotic authority, that nothing was wanting but the agitating presence of a bold and desperate leader, to precipitate the infected mass into the solid form of a concrete despotism.* And the present war has

---

* "I say to every man present, that there exists not on the face of the earth to-day a deeper nor a darker despotism than now reigns over the Southern people."— *Speech of Gen. Corcoran on Boston Common, Aug. 25th,* 1862.

"I had no idea that the whole people of a county could be so frightened as to permit a few men like Walter Mitchell and Wm. B. Stone and their confederates to create a reign of terror in their midst. But such was the

followed as naturally and as necessarily as darkness follows the setting of the natural sun. And
the present war must last, with all its world-
rocking commotions and its local devastation, till
one or the other of the conflicting principles,
either despotism or democracy, with its final adherents, no longer survives with power to carry
on the conflict. When the Southern leaders tell
us (and no Southern man, except their leaders,
ever tells us anything, except what has been put
into his mouth) that they have been forced into
this fight, they tell the truth. And the trueness
of the statement arises on this wise: From the
moulding force of slavery, or, to speak with more
definiteness, from the moulding force of their
perilous mastership, acting in their education,
their characters have become stamped with every
lineament of despotism, and their interests, so
far as they are able to discern where they lie,
are identified with the perpetuity of that hoary
crime. Hence the presence of an antagonist so
inimical as a free, self-governing people, vital
with the spirit of their civil institutions, and

fact : the people were so frightened, that it would have been impossible to
have raised fifty men in the whole county to fight the few rebel soldiers in
Port Tobacco."— *Private Letter from Charles Co., Md., Aug. 12th,* 1862.

"The Confederates once whipped in Virginia, and you will hear one prolonged and thundering shout for the downfall of this damnable government
from New Orleans to Fortress Monroe."— *Private Letter from Charleston,
S. C., July 20th,* 1862.

shining with success, necessitates this war, and
will continue so to do till one or the other of the
hostile parties is converted or consumed.

This necessity for a state of war has arisen,
not from any change that has taken place in the
North; not from anything the Northern people
have done; but from the Southern leaders, who
act for the Southern people, having become re-
converted back from democracy to despotism,
and seduced to repudiate the principles and to
subvert the institutions of their fathers by the
increasing profitableness of holding slaves.

XX.

Such being the educational power of mastership to transform the Democrat into a Despot,
it follows that before the free institutions of our
government can prevail again over its former
territorial limits, not only must that source of
the pernicious education become extinct, but
another generation of Southerners must be educated under different auspices. How effectually
the few years of the present war may avail to
displace the generation of its authors from mor-
tal life, from political and social power, and to
correct the vicious educating of those who are
to succeed them in the leading places of Southern politics and society, is a question that time
alone can answer. It is not, as the London
"Times" affirms, that "the United States must do
as Britain did in 1783, or govern the South as
Russia governs Poland." The "Times," that vile,
subsidized tool of despots, knows, if it would
admit, that the United States occupy the same

10*   118

position now which they occupied in 1783, as
the representatives and champions of free government; and now, as then, the antagonistic
arms of despotism must yield before them, if
the "Times" and its august compeers cannot
succeed in lying them into such a state of fear
and uncertainty as to give up the contest.

But we have not done with the practical detail of slave-holding, as it acts to mould the character and habits of the master.

To say that it confers a habit of command, is
to describe but a part of that ingrained sense of
superiority, that perfect contour of lordliness,
which results from lifelong surveillance over a
subject race, and which has in it much that com-
mands respect and exerts influence among men,
despite the absence of merit, of learning, and of
mental grasp, and the presence of much that is
mean, cruel, treacherous, dishonest, and unjust.
It acts instinctively and powerfully to place its
possessor above your criticism, above your investigation, and to command your reverend acquiescence without consulting your judgment or
your will. It can never be attained by study or
assumed by direct effort. It can never be generated or preserved in a democratic state of
society. It must be conferred from infancy,

doubtless becomes more or less hereditary, and acts with the spontaneous, instinctive ease, not of a second nature, but of a first. It results from lifelong habits of the successful exercise of dictatorial control over men. It enables its possessor to take the first move, the vantage ground, the choice of position, and contributes greatly toward his success in all transactions with those who have it not. This kind of superiority, when possessed by only an individual or family, has produced immense effects in the Old World; but when it comes to be the common heritage of an indefinitely extended class, as in this country, its full influence remains to be discovered. It has inclined and enabled Southern leaders so to husband the few political advantages they possessed, and so to turn their very weakness to advantage, that they have not only put a perpetual quietus upon all movements and tendencies contrary to their own among their own seven and three-fourths millions of poor white population, but to exercise a controlling influence in our national affairs, over Northern majorities and a predominance of learning, talent, truth, justice, and consistency. So that said Southern leaders have had their way in everything desired but in preventing the material progress and multiplying numbers of the Free States; and when they

found that, by virtue of dead weight, the North
was becoming too vast for them to handle, they,
by virtue of the quality we are considering, selected their own time and method and circumstances for terminating their connection with it.
But, thanks to an overruling Providence, they
have let the matter of separation alone too long.
Although overreached, befooled, and betrayed,
and although we commenced this contest with
a national treasury robbed and bankrupted, arsenals rifled of their contents, an army and navy
demoralized and depressed, and their remnants
scattered to the ends of the earth; though the
national administration, for the first time composed practically of Northern men, without an
element of the hitherto all-controlling Southern
leadership to give it strength, cannot conceal its
weakness; and although, from the commencement of the war to the time of this writing, September 12, 1862, our commanders in the field
appear to have been, on the whole, extensively
outgeneralled and baffled by that same disdain-
ful assuming of the initiative on the part of their
antagonists, which has baffled our congressmen
for half a century, — yet we expect, and not
without good reason, that by mere dead weight,
superiority of numbers and resources, we shall
triumph in the end.

It was this quality of Southern leadership, the result of being born and educated masters, which petulant Northern journalists, notwithstanding the wonderful power which it exerts, and the success of its applications, persist in denominating "superciliousness," and "insufferable insolence," that inclined and enabled the South Carolina legislature with impunity to mob the agent (Judge Hoar) of Massachusetts sent to prosecute a case in the United States court at their capital, — that inclined and enabled Preston S. Brooks with impunity to cudgel Senator Sumner in his senatorial chair till a trifle more of the same treatment would have terminated his life, — that enabled Andrew Jackson to demolish the United States Bank, and virtually to terminate the application of Federal appropriations to purposes of internal improvement; and, under pretence of "conscientious scruples" and "constitutional objections," with others like him, his compeers and successors, to do whatever they deemed best adapted to cripple the strength and impede the prosperity of the Northern States, — to establish a compromise line, bounding slave territory on the North, when they thought such action for their advantage, and abolish it when they saw fit, — to resort to the doctrine of popular sovereignty to abolish the Missouri Compromise, thereby bringing Kansas into dispute, between Free State and Pro-slavery parties, and to resort to a military despotism to force slavery into it as soon as it had become disputable, — so perpetually to dictate the policy of the general government as to inhibit all acknowledgment of nationality at home or abroad, in Liberia, Hayti, or elsewhere, to any people of the races from whom their slaves are taken, — so to dictate at the North the sentiments with which negroes shall be regarded, as to exclude them from the common rights of citizens and from military service, at the imminent risk of losing all we have at stake in the present war, in consequence of that exclusion.

XXI.

OTHER TRAITS OF CHARACTER CONFERRED BY HIS POSITION ON THE SLAVE-MASTER, FITTING HIM FOR WAR; AND DISPLAYED BY HIS CLASS IN THE PRESENT CONTEST.

ASIDE from the quality mentioned in the last chapter as resulting from lifelong presiding over a servile race, there are other qualities, or traits of character, acquired thereby, and not often derived from any other source. Among these is a certain wakeful, watchful, reconnoitring alertness, an instinctive, habitual quickness to apprehend danger, and effectually to provide against it, the result of being born and bred in a state of perpetual war, where tremendous penalties for remissness were continually pending.

What! it will be asked by some, is the state of the slave-holder a state of perpetual war? The answer to this inquiry is, Yes. And the only qualification needed to explain the answer is, that the "master race" is, in general, in a state of complete triumphant success; so that very little fighting has to be done. The only reason that there is not frequent and active fighting is, that the negroes are effectually deprived of means and opportunities to fight with the remotest probability of success. That there is just and sufficient cause for constant war, the negro and his master alike well know. It is the discipline and practice of keeping his negroes thus perpetually deprived of the means and opportunities of waging active war, that gives the slave-holder the habit, and at length the power, of examining, measuring, estimating, and comprehending every man that presents himself for acquaintance, or for transactions with him : that is, he measures, estimates. and comprehends him so far as to arrive at an approximately certain conclusion as to what course of action he is likely to pursue, what benefits or mischiefs are likely to accrue to himself (the slave-holder) and to his cause therefrom, and how, and how far, it becomes incumbent on him to make provision against such mischiefs.

The slave-holder also understands and acts on the importance of tampering with his enemy, to bribe and disarm his hostile feeling, and thereby lessen the danger and the frequency of resistful encounters. Every time he corrects a servant for misbehavior, he fights an engagement in the general perpetual battle, by complete success in which on the part of the master the negro race are kept against their wills in implicit and profitable servitude. Another lesson, eminently fitting one for active war, which the master of slaves is compelled to learn, is to take care of himself. The war he is perpetually engaged in carrying on is not a war with equals; it is war with a servile race; and in such a war it would be disgracefully imprudent to allow himself to be injured. Hence the purpose to inflict a punishment, or to transfer by sale, or anything that is likely to rouse the negro to resistance, is instinctively kept an inscrutable secret; the negro is eyed and calculated for till it is seen that he is about to come into a position where he can be captured, handcuffed, and handled at pleasure, and without peril to the master.

Hence the sly, secret, stealthy operations of the Southern forces in the existing war, and their persistent and perpetual refusal to fight, except where overwhelming numbers, or advantageous position, or some other advantage on their side appears to them to place their success beyond a question; also their unparalleled and inimitable indifference to what all other warriors have esteemed to be the disgrace of fleeing before the face of an equal foe. Hence, too, their torpedoes by land and sea, their bushwhacking, their assassination of pickets, picking off officers

11

in engagements, and the like, — proceedings which have been criticised and complained of by Northern men as " outrageous," " mean," and " treacherous," but which result necessarily from the lifelong education every Southern master has received. Hence, also, the noteworthy success of the South in taking prisoners. Though whipped in three or four battles, where they are victors in one, they take more than prisoners enough to exchange for all they lose.

Efficiency of action is another trait that has become confirmed, and, to a great extent, perfected, in the character of the slave-holders as a class. It arises from the tremendous penalties of failure in dealing with their negroes, which penalties are continually hanging over them, and from habits of complete success which have for ages attended their labors for the subjugation of the Africans. Extremely few experiments are ever tried by this class of men. Hence their notorious destitution of any spirit of invention, and the exceeding slowness with which they admit the most important and most demonstrated improvements 'of the age.

This habit of decisive action, as displayed by them in inaugurating and carrying on the present war, has been remarked and wondered at, ridiculed and doubted, by observers in and out

of authority in the North, and in Europe. It
was thought by some to augur something in
favor of the South in reference to the final result, and was regarded for a time by all as characteristic of this particular contest. But it is a
characteristic habit of Southern leaders, a class
of men who, from educational causes above-men-
tioned, never accept of partial success unless it
be temporarily, and as a means of achieving
complete and final triumph in the end.

Language is feeble to portray that absolute
determinedness not only to succeed or perish,
but not to be defeated when one has perished,
which becomes habitual to the leading Southern
mind as a necessary result of a lifelong contem-
plation of the imminent and enormous perils of
failure in dealing with a body of three or four
millions of slaves, valuable and intelligent, and
daily increasing in value and intelligence, and in
disposition and in power to be free. The present onslaught on the national existence, vast as
is the scale of its operations, presents but a feeble *exposé* of the infernal force that has been
gendered and will be matured by a few generations more of a limited class of slave-holders
being permitted to bear the responsibilities and
ply the functions of their vocation in the bosom
of this otherwise democratic republic. If the

Northern people or the national administration choose to carry on war with these men as an experiment, to see whether their character and purpose will not change under the operation, they can do so ; but it will be an experiment of transcendent costliness, and the issue of that war will be dictated by this unbending trait of Southern character. With an utterly inexhaustible fund of patient mildness on the side of the government, — a mildness that refuses to exterminate anything, even for the salvation of its own confiding, imperilled, impoverished, tormented and tortured dependents, — and on the other side a relentless decisiveness as utterly unchanging ; exhaustless resources on the part of the former combatant can only prolong the war, and postpone a catastrophe which those resources cannot finally avert.

XXII.

ONE important point has been implied in the
previous pages, which has not been explained.

We have spoken of the despotic character acquired by the master in dealing with his slaves,
as if the same would still attach to him in his
dealings with white people, — we have spoken
of the peculiarities of the particular modes of
warfare by which he maintains his victorious supremacy over the negro race, as if these same peculiarities would still characterize him in his war
against the free North in pursuit of the liberty
of holding other men in bondage.

Now the Southerners and their Northern
friends will strenuously protest against this mode
of reasoning. They will maintain most ear-
nestly that they never intended to treat gentle-
men, or white people, in anything like the way
in which they are obliged to treat the blacks.
A few months ago, this kind of talk sounded

well, and gained believing listeners; and the danger is, that a few months hence, being sauced with a good deal of Southern blandishment, and seasoned with a spice of concealed Northern treason, it will again be urged on the Northern government and people with some success, namely, that men have one character in their dealings with black men, and another in their dealings with white men, — that they may be the rankest despots in their dealings with negroes, and the most sincere of democrats in all their relations to the whites. We shall, doubtless, be told presently that it was altogether an oversight, repented of and apologized for, that during the heat of the contest their ideas became somewhat mixed, and in language, in deeds, and in bitter violence of feeling, "they unfortunately identified us with the despised negroes. And this too, only so far as they supposed themselves to have just cause to believe that we placed ourselves on a level with the negroes, and were really employed in aiding them to secure their liberty by a servile war."

Two considerations stand in the way of all this. First we are not dealing with the admitted intentions of slave-holders, or of any other men. We are contemplating their characters, the laws that govern their actions, that have governed them heretofore, and will govern them hereafter, whether the performers of those actions intelligently design it or not ; and never more legitimately than during the din of conflict, when customary disguises and artificial restraints are necessarily forgotten, and the roused individual displays his true self with more sincere honesty than it would have been possible for him to practise, had he not been thrown entirely off his guard by the fire and strifes of war. These sincere traits of character, these laws that have governed and still must govern their undisguised conduct, were displayed by guerrilla warfare, masked batteries, assassination of pickets, poisoning springs, and selling poisoned provisions to our soldiers, sequestration of the property of Union Southerners, persecution, imprisonment, and hanging, of such Unionists, sinking infernal machines to blow up our ships on the water, and planting torpedoes to mutilate and murder unsuspecting men on land, plundering and disrobing our dead on the battle-field, robbing the wounded of their haversacks and leaving them to die by starvation; disinterring our dead to get their skulls for drinking-cups and their bones for relics, treating prisoners with wanton outrage and cruelty, and shooting them down in cold blood, — these, and a volume more of like transactions perpetrated by the Rebels in this War, verify beyond dispute, that the distinction made by slave-holders between white and black in the putting forth of their democratic or despotic principles and modes of action, is a purely fictitious and fanciful distinction, and wherever it is observed at all, it is so observed only for lack of power to enforce the cruel dictates of their tyrannical principles and habits, and the desire of their Africanized, barbarous hearts.

The truth is, — and this is the second objection we bring against the pretended reasoning of the slave-holders and their friends, — that the principles and habits of despotism are supreme and all-moulding in their possessor. He cannot rid himself of their all-controlling force. As well might you plant a tree with all its roots aboveground, and all its leafy boughs beneath the sod, and expect it to flourish and bear fruit; as well might you take a child of the ordinary human stock, in full health, and make him promise and swear not to grow to exceed three feet three inches in stature, and not to exceed fifty pounds in weight, as expect a man who has been born and bred to the exercise of despotic control over men, to lay by the principles and practices of despotism, and become an honest democratic member of a democratic community. He may

become such a member of such a community;
but it will be only in submission to a force that
utterly precludes the possibility of his doing otherwise.   And the moment that compelling, coercive force is relaxed, that moment, as a perfectly elastic physical body, released from the
force that had compressed it, springs again into
its full former form and dimensions, so the coer-
cively democratized despot will instinctively
spring again into the exercise of his former
despotic principles and habits, all the purposes
he may have formed, all the promises he may
have made, and all the oaths he may have
taken, to the contrary notwithstanding.

Not only is it the law of the human mind, —
a law admitting of no exceptions, other than
such as are made by compulsive force, — that
despots will deal despotically; but it is also such
a law that they will do so ultimately, to the full
extent of their ability, to the utmost limits of
the population over whom they are able to establish their control.   And the idea that our
Southern despots, having three or four millions
of blacks under their unquestioned control,
would bound their exercise of and their greed
for power, by the line that limits the complex-
ion of the African skin, is one of the shallow-

est fallacies with which a rational man ever un-
took to deceive himself.

Like the facility with which wealth is accumulated, so the ease of accumulating despotic
power increases in geometrical ratio to what is
already possessed.

Had the Southern tyrants had no supreme
control over millions of blacks, they could never
have subjugated the seven and three-fourths
millions of poor white population. Had they
not succeeded in establishing an absolute despotic control over these millions of non-slave-
holding whites in the Southern States, they would
not have been able to entail on the North these
years of bloody and exhausting war for the
enlargement and perpetuation of their despotic
sway.

When the framers of the Constitution guaran-
teed to slave-holders the perpetual, quiet possession of their increasing numbers of African
slaves, they put into the hands of that class of
men a weapon wherewith they could presently
put that Constitution, with all its beneficent
provisions, out of existence. When the rise of
the cotton-trade gave new vitality and pecuniary power to slave-holders, it necessarily imparted to them the disposition and the power
to use that weapon.

If the present war does not deprive slave-holding of permanent vitality, so that it can never take root and sprout into vigorous growth again, then the present war will act on the causes that produced it, only as a limited amount of water acts on a conflagration which it suffices only to deaden, while it does not quench.

The slave-holders and their apologizing friends tell us that " the abolitionists are the cause of the present war." Every man who refuses to bow his neck in permanent subjection to the Southern despots whom slavery has raised up, is the cause of this war by said refusal. If the whole Northern population had so bowed their necks, then would there have been no war, and on no other condition. On any other condition than that perpetual and universal submission on the part of the whole Northern population to be ruled over by the masters of the Southern slaves, the present war will rage, and must inevitably rage, in one form or another, and at longer or shorter intervals, till either despotism or democracy is exterminated from within our country's boundaries.

Whether the genus Despot can be preserved and propagated by the subject class of the Southern despotism, is a question on which there need be no doubt or controversy. The change of place from the subject to the dominant class in a despotic community, is a natural and easy change. And unless the blacks and whites of the subject class in the Southern States are elevated to the rank, and inspired with the principles of equals among equals in a democratic community, as sure as that the dead carcass breeds worms, so sure is it that the dominant class will not long be wanting, and the despotic form of Southern society will be preserved, with more or less detriment and peril to the democratic North. And those Northern-born and Northern-bred politicians who are laboring with intense persistency, by opposing the emancipation war policy, to conserve the interests of self-immolated slave-holders, are thereby doing all that God has placed it in their power to do, to forge and fasten on their own posterity, and on all the freemen of the North, the same inhuman despotism, which, at this hour is submitting to every Southern white man between the ages of sixteen and forty-five (sixty in some states), who is not the owner of twenty slaves, the cool alternative of placing himself in the front of a deadly fight for destroying the government of his fathers, or among those who are being led out by scores, and shot down like dogs, for not obeying their leaders.*

* CINCINNATI, Sept. 15, 1863. The *Gazette* has a Leavenworth despatch which says: " Gen. Blunt at last accounts was at Fort Gibson, preparing to start for Fort Scott. Refugees from the rebel conscription are coming into Blunt's lines by hundreds. Their sufferings are represented as indescribable. More than one hundred Union men have been shot and hung at Fort Smith since the rebellion begun." The Nashville *Union* of the 6th October, 1863, says: "It is not known, we believe, that the privilege of *habeas corpus* has been suspended *altogether* in the Confederacy, for over twelve months. We have the highest judicial authority for stating this fact, although we cannot give any name. The suspension was made by a private order of Jeff. Davis to the leading judicial officers, and never has been published. Probably not one man in fifty thousand in all Rebeldom is aware that for over twelve months, the privilege of *habeas corpus* has not existed in the South at all. Our authority on this point, we repeat, is unquestionable." A volume might be filled with similar accounts.

XXIII.

WE have now considered in detail, to the extent proposed, the operation of slavery as it has existed since the change that was wrought in it after the adoption of the Constitution; namely, its operation to convert back to despotism the sons of sires who fought, bled, toiled, and sacrificed, without remission and without reserve, to win the independence of our common country, and to establish within it the glorious fabric of free government, an achievement which has brought more of hope and joy and of substantial happiness to the human family than any other event that has occurred since the dawn of time, except the advent of the Christ of God.

We have seen that slavery, in its modern form, necessarily concentrates such an enormous amount of imperilled interest, antagonistic to everything that pertains to freedom, as would overthrow a stronger government than ours, had not the potent cause of freedom rapidly and gloriously accumulated to itself an amount of population and resources that wellnigh outweighs the available resources of the remaining portion of the world. We have seen that, in addition to vast pecuniary interest, the loose luxuriance of a semi-barbarous state of society, the intoxicating sweets of despotic sway, and a powerful practical predominance in all national affairs, — all which to their possessors depend on the maintenance of the slave system, — the dreaded horrors of slave insurrection are perpetually impending, to enforce on the "master class" a unity of purpose, a harmony of action, a subjugating of every voluntary power to the one ruling necessity, which is, of itself, the highest, strongest, form of despotism. We have seen that lifelong compliance with this enforced necessity of despotic action must mould and fashion the character of the slave-holder, whether he will or not, with all the features of a despot.

We have seen that the habit of command, if that term be used to cover the attendant peculiarities of the habit it describes, together with the advantages resulting to them from their own enforced unity of action and concentration of interest, has inclined and enabled a few thousand slave-holders, not only to mould and manage their own seven and three-fourths millions of non-slave-holding white population, like potters' clay, but, in the legislative, executive, and judicial branches of our national government, to do everything they could desire, except fatally to suppress the rapid increase of numbers and material prosperity at the North.

We have seen that, aside from the direct effect of slave-holding to despotize the principles and habits of the master, the influence of negro associations from youth to hoary age, from generation to generation, must have a powerful effect, in his comparative seclusion from other society, to depress and barbarize the standard of his civilization,— thus giving powerful collateral aid to his natural lust for gain and lust for despotic power ; also to disincline and unfi him to return to the political preferences and affections of his fathers, and to do away with the compunctions he might otherwise be supposed to have, for using the despotic power he possessed in a barbarous way and for barbarous purposes.

A state of war is perfectly normal to a despotism. It is the reverse of this to a democracy. So much so, that even democratic material has to be thrown into grades of subordinate and commander, and the whole placed under a despotic head, before it can be called an army, or become at all reliable for fighting purposes. We have seen that a state of mastership over a subject race, as the negro race is held in the Southern States in recent years, is, and necessarily must be, a state of war, and calls into constant and vigorous exercise all those accomplishments of strategy, re-connoissance, inscrutable reticence, and decisive action, which are the highest attainments of the warlike leader; while the act of corporal pun-ishment, which must be perpetually pending, and more or less frequently performed, serves to brutalize the finer feelings, and divest the state of actual war of much of the repugnance with which it would necessarily present itself to other classes of society.

XXIV.

IT has been stated in the foregoing pages of
this work, that despotism and democracy, slavery and free government, are inimical to each
other,— that exterminating hostility must rage
between them till one or the other perishes,
wherever they coexist.

This is not a mere antagonism of abstract
principles. The antagonism of principle works
itself out in concrete form; and the different
steps of its operation are not too secret to be
uncovered and explained.

In no respect is this overt antagonism more
apparent than in the military qualities which
despotism imparts, the military grades it im-
poses, the military strength it relies upon, and
the military spirit and habits which it produces;
while the action of democracy is the reverse of
this in every particular.

In monarchical government, the whole reli-

188

ance for securing immunity from an invasion of
national territory or rights is military strength,
which bids defiance to the power that threatens
wrong. As soon as wrong is threatened, military qualities are put in action to forestall the
execution of that threat; whereas, in the democratic community, the principle acted on is, that
if there is no tension, there will be no rupture;
if there is no compression, there will be no explosion. Entirely occupied in developing their
own resources of peace, the people of a democratic community naturally judge others by
themselves, and suppose that every civil community is so employed. They think little of
the need of defence, and have no motive to
assail. Peace is to them so much more profitable than war, they are slow to believe that
other nations regard their interest in a different
light. Indeed, it is no small source of their felt
security, that from their example of affluence,
and from the lucrativeness of their commerce, it
is really more profitable for their neighbor to be
at peace than to be at war with them. The
very contagion of their open, tolerant, and un-
warlike feeling exerts no small influence to
keep other nations from aggression. From the
very constitution of society, organically des-
titute of a watchful head or leaders who feel

themselves habitually responsible for the welfare of the whole, it is almost impossible to
alarm a democratic community; and still more
difficult to obtain effective action, where action
depends on the spontaneously harmonious movement of the headless and disintegrated mass.
And when the democratic people do move for
military effect, it is only by an abandoning of
their characteristic state and modes of action,
and adopting those of despotism, to such an extent as to incur some danger that they will not,
when war is over, readily return to democratic
form. And were the object fought for any other
than to repel an assault on their civil liberties,
the danger would be imminent, that free principles would be affected unfavorably by their
course of action. So that in addition to the
peril of being subjugated by military force, such
is the repugnance of a state of civil freedom to
a state of war that a democratic government is
in imminent peril of being worried out of existence as a democracy, by the perpetual menace
and irritation of a despotic institution within
its boundaries, or a despotic government located
on its borders.

Such a despotic government on its border,
having, as all neighboring governments have, or
suppose themselves to have, continually, some

causes of complaint against its neighbor, and naturally and necessarily resorting to military menace to obtain redress and secure future respect, thereby forces on its democratic neighbor the necessity of frequently abandoning her natural modes of action, of sensibly interrupting the lucrative employments of her citizens, to assume a warlike attitude and assume the grading and the drill, and take up the weapons, of despotism to repel threatened assault.

So great is the peril from this source that under the supervision of divine Intelligence, no permanently democratic government came into existence until a whole broad continent had been prepared and set apart for its development, with broad and effective ocean barriers on every side between it and the nearest despotic power. And the practical success of ocean steam navigation, which has brought the opposite shores of these barrier waters so near together, was not permitted to take place until the democratic power on this continent had passed the perils of its infancy. If leading Southerners or their allies and abettors, the monarchists of Europe, are aiming, through the unguardedness of the present national administration, or the so-called Democratic party of the North, to subvert and finally ruin the democratic institutions of this country, as they doubtless very well understand, nothing else is necessary to that result but the recognition of a Southern government, founded on slavery as its capital institution.

XXV.

SAME GENERAL SUBJECT CONTINUED — THE POOR WHITES OF
A SLAVE-HOLDING COMMUNITY EQUIVALENT TO A STAND-
ING ARMY, WHEN CONTRASTED WITH THE DESTITUTION OF
COMBATANTS WHICH MARKS A DEMOCRACY.

THE overt antagonism of monarchy to free
government, bodied forth by the slave interest
in the South, against the active freedom of the
Northern portion of this country, is, perhaps, in
nothing more apparent than in the idleness it
induces in the great majority of the Southern
whites. This is done, in part, by rendering labor
disreputable, — throwing a stench of servility, an
air of degradation, about industrial pursuits, followed for the honest earning of one's livelihood.

It is done, in part, by rendering labor unne-
cessary to the whites. The mild climate, with
scarcely any winter, reduces the list of absolutely
necessary things for one to live on, to a very
small number and amount. The abundance
with which these are produced, under a Southern sun, makes them easily attained. The great
profit of slave-labor leaves much to be disposed
of by the slave-holder gratuitously to friends

and dependents, and semi-gratuitously to all who
need. The characteristic and habitually easy
handling, by the masters, of what their negroes
earn, serves to throw an odor of niggardliness on
the small earnings and savings of one who works
with his own hands. The same result is still
farther promoted by the monopolizing of the
land, and of the production of the great staples
of trade by the wealthy slave-owner, leaving
very scanty resources for the white man to
spend his industry on, unless he goes with the
negroes into the field, for negro wages, which
almost none will do.

The result is, that the poor whites, who constitute the immense majority of the whole Southern population, lie perpetually in unconfined
idleness, with nothing to lose, and little to
fear, from any change of circumstances; ever
ready, at the shortest notice, to be constituted
into a military force, without pay or rations,
to be precipitated upon any offending or unoffending neighbor, at the option of their natural
leaders, the slave-holders; thus constituting a
force but few removes from a standing army,
perpetually menacing those, who, being democrats, must necessarily be hated by the despotic
slave-holders.

The full force of this standing menace is not

perceived until the peculiar character of the community against which it is directed is brought to view. It is a community of preëminently industrious, thriving, individuals. The pressure of dictatorial authority, and its hampering institutions, has long since been removed. With almost the freedom of the savage state are combined the refined enlightenment, the upward aspirations, and the susceptibility of being injured, peculiar to the highest civilization. The humblest individual in that community, excepting a few who are a prey to rare vices or misfortunes, has the prospect of easy competency, and an open road, if he chooses to follow it, to positions of the highest social eminence. The consequence is, that there is hardly a class, however small, who can be spared to take up arms, and meet the standing menace of the South. Whoever does this has, in most instances, to leave a suffering family and a neglected business. Our own merchant marine cannot be manned without drawing largely on the aid of foreigners. Except a few for officers, our native-born citizens can be better employed. When the worst has come, and an army must be raised to defend the North, in the absence of despotic coercion to enforce sacrifice, enormous outlays must be incurred in wages, bounties, subsistence, and pensions, to fill

13

the army ranks with men, who are accustomed
to every comfort, and to the enjoyment of more
or less accumulated and still accumulating wealth.
Aside from the enormous public expense, to
induce the enlistment of these men, and the
pecuniary sacrifice that many of them still make
by enlisting, they feel it to be a great sacrifice
to leave their quiet and happy homes, for the
perils and privations inseparable from a campaign; whereas, the Southern ranks, by a simple
authoritative decree, are filled with men who
have nothing to leave, and nothing to peril, but
the semi-enjoyment of a degraded, ignorant, and
poverty-stricken existence, by being drafted into
a Southern army, without pay, subsistence, or
clothing, to any considerable amount, beyond
what they can supply themselves with, or plunder from friends or foes,* and all at the bid of
despots whose dictation they are almost " un-
gifted with any ability to resist," — The North,

---

* " Many a Northern man, of the pickets especially, has been killed for
his clothes."—*Army correspondent.*

A correspondent of the Lowell *News*, who has lately escaped from Savannah, tells the following story : —

" After the assault on Fort Wagner, when Colonel Shaw was killed, a
rebel soldier was showing his boots in Savannah, and bragging how he got
them. He said he attempted to take them off a Yankee soldier on that fatal
field, who, though wounded, remonstrated, saying there were dead ones
enough from whom he might take a pair. Then, with a fiendish exultation,
he went on to say how he thought he wouldn't rob the wounded, so, putting
his bayonet through the man's heart, he took the boots and came away. If
devils ever dance, that fellow should be counted in, boots and all."

at the same time, not only having no competent
leaders, but, from the construction and habits of
its society, being almost incapable of producing
leaders competent to conduct its affairs, in a
state of war, to any satisfactory result.

Under these circumstances, aside from the in-
delible disgrace, enfeeblement, and humiliation,
of parting with a needed portion of our national
domain, to permit the establishment of a slave-
holding confederacy on the borders of this republic would be about as bald a suicide as a
nation of idiots could commit.

A perpetual series of alarms, which the leaders of such a confederacy would instinctively
be raising, at no cost to themselves, and for mere
amusement, would, in a few years, worry the
Northern democratic government out of existence, by keeping it in a state of afflicted uncertainty, more disastrous to its delicate and varied
industrial and commercial interests than actual
war. No sane man can pretend that treaties
with such a confederacy would avail any more
than did the official oaths of the traitor senators,
congressmen, and cabinet officers, who gendered
it.

XXVI.

In the light of the foregoing reflections, we are, perhaps, prepared to make some just estimate of the real and immediate causes of the existing war. In attempting to do so, we find that natural history is encroaching more nearly than before on the boundaries of history proper; and the natural causes which we have hitherto been tracing in their action, irrespectively of any human design or intelligent purpose, will henceforth be bodying themselves forth in the intelligent purpose and resolute action of the prime movers of this nefarious Rebellion.

Slavery, as we now are called to look upon it, has advanced from the state of unimportance and of non-influence in which it did not interfere with the declaration of our independence, or the adoption of our national Constitution, in 1776–'89, to a condition of all-moulding influence and incalculable pecuniary importance, in 1860. It

148

has moulded Southern society into the grades of despotism. It has reduced the mass of non-slave-holding whites to a state of degraded ignorance and poverty, bereft of any capacity or disposition to controvert the authority of anybody who may assume, to dictate to them. It has, by its necessary action, moulded the sentiments and habits of the master, to the purest, fiercest form of despotism, reversing the democratic character and devotion of his illustrious sires, and putting him under the pressure of pecuniary and social influences adequate to dispel all hesitancy as to maintaining his present position. He has retained just enough of democracy to serve as a rule of harmonious action between himself and his fellow-despots, as they serve together, with one heart and one mind, in profound obedience to the dictates of their one consolidated interest. The practice of holding slaves has conferred on him almost all the qualities of a military strategist and leader, in a high degree; has done much to divest him of any aversion to a state of war, and he has become conscious of his irresponsible sway over the mass of poor whites in his own section.

The practice of slave-holding has also conferred on the master the faculty of controlling, and its stringent necessities have supplied him with an efficient motive to control the policy, and, to a great extent, the action, in detail, of the general government.

The question here presents itself, demanding to be answered, whether natural causes, at this time, necessitated a precipitation of the armed conflict. Had the antagonistic principle of despotism, as prevailing at the South, so far expressed itself in overt injury and annoyance as to force the North into armed resistance? Or had the material and numerical progress of the North rendered it unsafe for the South longer to count on her forbearance?

Looking at the question from a Northern position, and with the mild, tolerant eye of a Democrat, there was, at this time, no necessity of a rupture. Innocently supposing others to be as open and honest as themselves, fully occupied by their several schemes of individual aggrandizement, the Northern politicians had never extended their investigations so far as to discover that there was working in the South a governmental principle, potent, vital, and aggressive, inimical to their spirit and practices of freedom. That the Constitution bound them to non-interference with slavery in the States was universally admitted. And had the South been satisfied with this, and with the lenient exercise of their own predominance in the general administration, no class or number of alarmists could have roused the North to acts of overt hostility.

But look at the same question from a Southern point of view, with the eye of a tyrant's jealousy and suspicion, as he stands surrounded by the imminent and enormous perils of servile insurrectionary disturbance, beneath the shadow of a vast and growing governmental force, imbued with the spirit of democracy, and necessarily inimical to the despotic system which he has wrapped about him till he could not rid himself of it if he would, and a different answer had to be given. To wield the political influence, and to conserve the interests of concentrated slavery, devolved on men who never trusted in anything which they could not control, never asked for anything which they could not exact, never commended any course of action which they could not compel. Their character was the necessary result of their education. Hardly anybody, that had not been trained on the deck of a pirate or of a slave-ship, could be expected to comprehend their motives, or to predict their course of action.

XXVII.

ALTHOUGH, in the early history of the government, the Southern or Slave States outweighed
the North in territorial extent and population,
yet it soon became apparent that the principles
of free government, as carried out at the North,
were operating to develop the resources of that
section to an unparalleled degree, and were securing to it almost the entire influx of foreign population. Its territorial expansion, which could
not be checked, could only be equalled for a
time by a forced expansion on the part of the
South.

This constantly augmenting preponderance
on the part of the North never escaped the notice or due consideration of leading Southerners. They were for thirty years counting on
the hour when their domination in the general
government would be hopelessly outweighed,
and the temporizing shifts to which they long

resorted to keep up their practical predominance could no longer be relied on. They had
taken these thirty years to deliberate on the
course they would pursue in the foreseen emergency; with characteristic reticence they had
concealed their conclusion, and taken all the
preparatory steps necessary to carry their purpose into execution. The repugnance that existed between their own system and what they
were sometimes pleased to call the "agrarianism"* of the North, they had deeply pondered
and justly weighed.

The continued coexistence of the two antagonistic forces within the limits of one government, they never were stupid enough to expect.

From the time that the profitable expansion
of the business of producing cotton became
an admitted fact, they had turned their backs
irrevocably on all projects looking toward emancipation, or toward any considerable relaxation
of the rigor of the slave-system as then practised.

* The practical abandonment of those class distinctions without which
a monarchical form of society has no existence. And, as a real monarchist
never admits, never even conceived of, the existence of government without sovereigns, one or more, "agrarianism" is a mild expression to describe the anarchy, the utter absence of all government, which he necessarily supposes to exist where there is no governing class.

Nothing remained to them but prospective separation from the Federal Union.*

Men of their antecedents and surroundings, of their character, and in their circumstances, could have come to no other conclusion. Nothing remained contingent but the time and mode of bringing the separation about. Thus the minds of leading Southern men were educated for a generation under the influence of the deliberate purpose to establish a separate Southern government. Nor was this the educating influence of a mere idle purpose. The revolution that separated Texas from Mexico was a bold and successful step, planned and executed by Southern adventurers in aid of that design. The subsequent admission of Texas to the Union, the consequent war with Mexico, and the acquisition of New Mexico, California, and Arizona, were all so many successive steps brought about in obedience to the same design.

* Once out from under the national Constitution, with four or more millions of blacks in utter subjugation, and eight or more millions of whites whom they can shoot and hang with impunity, with half the former national territory and coast whereon to raise armies and navies, with the acknowledged right to make foreign alliances and treaties, without any natural boundary between their territory and the Northern States, these men never doubted their governmental ability to keep the North so perpetually in hot water, as effectually to check its material progress, and to teach its money-earning, money-saving population, that not only black men but white men "have no rights which" a slave-holding cotton lord "is bound to respect."

The incurring of enormous debts (perhaps only constructively) by the State of Texas, to certain of her citizens, and the subsequent assuming of these debts by the general government, constituted, perhaps, one of the first of a series of acts, designed to impoverish the North, or the general government, preparatory to the coming separation.

The writer of these pages was personally cognizant of the fact, that eighteen years before the civil disturbances in Kansas took place, under the administration of President Pierce, it was the plan of leading slave-holders to "bring the question of the extension of slavery, to an issue of arms on some territory external to the jurisdiction of any State government." It was presumed that Northern men would not fight, and that slight demonstrations of prowess on the part of Southerners would enable the latter to have matters all their own way. It was a refinement on this original design, to have the general government, in the hands of Southern men, with such an automaton as Frank Pierce in the executive chair, make armed demonstrations in behalf of slave extension, with a view, if possible, to betray the freedom-loving North into acts of overt hostility against the Federal government, and bring on a war against slavery, with the treasury, the authority, the army and navy of the general government on the Southern side in the conflict.

The outrages committed against the Free-State men and their property, lives, and families in Kansas, were not accidental; they were a part of the regular plan, ordered and insisted on from headquarters, in furtherance of the above design. But with the hanging of John Brown and his associates, this part of the programme failed; except so far as its prosecution had availed to ferment animosity between the Northern and Southern people; to supply material for misrepresenting the North in Southern sections, and to supply the occasion for getting up and exercising some martial spirit among the people of Virginia.*

Kindred to these operations for bringing the North into overt conflict with the general government, was the plan of packing the supreme bench of the United States Court, with a view to obtain decisions so outrageously violative of the principles of free-government, as to weary out the patience of the Northern people and exasperate them beyond control.

* It was of very great importance to the success of their subsequent designs, civil and military, that the Southern leaders should have this occasion to bring their own abject underlings through the surprise and repugnance of a first taking-up of arms.

This packing of the United States Court commenced as far back as the appointment of Roger B. Taney to a seat upon its bench, as a reward for his subserviency in removing the treasury deposits from the United States Bank, an act of doubtful legality, which his predecessor in the treasury department refused to do, in obedience to General Jackson's imperious and unreasonable mandate.

The framing of the Fugitive Slave Law, with features of needless harshness, was also planned with a view to irritate the North into acts of violence against the general government.

12*

XXVIII.

THE annexing of territory to the South and West, with a view to increase the territorial preponderance of the slave section, and favor the multiplication of Slave States, the depletion of the United States treasury, to add absolute and comparative wealth to the South, the bringing of the slavery controversy to an issue of arms on the territory, the planned and perpetrated enormities on the Free-State settlers in Kansas, and the needless harshness of the Fugitive Slave Law, with other like efforts to irritate the North into acts of overt hostility to the general government, while that government was yet in the hands of Southern leaders, and the packing of the United States Court, were all measures of secondary importance, compared with the grand scheme of corrupting, dividing, and preoccupying the North, by means of the so-called Democratic party. This qualified term is here used to designate this important political fraternity, not as an expression of disrespect, but because their favorite self-applied titles, Democracy and Democratic, cannot be here appropriated as they have been wont to use them, without doing irreparable violence to the vocabulary of history·

Soon after the close of the Revolutionary War, two great parties developed themselves among the constituency and leading statesmen of the Union. Difference of opinion and of preference, respecting the degree to which governmental power should be centralized in the general administration, to the disparagement of State organizations, appears to have been the chief ground of difference on which these party combinations first took their rise. With different degrees of intensity in the cohesion with which their several elements united, with some variety, and even interchange of the names by which, at different periods, these parties were severally designated, and with more or less change, from time to time, in the distinctive principles, or political creeds, on which they claimed to found the different courses of governmental action which they severally advocated, these two great political parties continued till the time of Jackson's administration.

This appears to have been, more than any

other, the period of a commencing transition in the condition of our national affairs, — a commencing transition from a state of comparative feebleness and peril to a state of conscious and defiant strength, — of commencing transition from a state of debt-incumbered national poverty and enforced economy to a state of conscious pecuniary ease and affluence, which, perhaps inevitably, begets looseness, extravagance, and corrupt procedures.

The individual character of President Jackson himself, also, had much to do with the impress his eight years' administration left on the country in general, and on the political party which sustained him in particular. Bold and energetic in the extreme, by birth and education a Southerner of the western type, proud of that frankness and honesty which does much to gild and give *eclat* even to the strongest vices, a soldier, accustomed to camp habits and successful campaigns, he never shrunk from the assumption of any responsibility which he thought there was occasion to exercise; confessedly a stranger to any higher virtues than unbounded devotion to his friends, and an exterminating vindictiveness toward those whom he viewed as enemies, perhaps the most remarkable feature of his character was an unguarded susceptibility of being imposed upon by those who succeeded in maintaining in his presence a friendly attitude.

His bold, frank, energetic, and decided character gave confidence and strength to his political adherents, who never allowed themselves to be embarrassed with cumbering creeds, or political doctrines, that did not work well for the time being; his military renown proved to be a profitable basis on which to erect political reputation; his gallant quashing of South Carolina's insane and ill-timed attempt at nullifying the acts of the general government, by an assumption of supreme power on behalf of the individual State, made him stand well at the North, while his supreme rule of favoring his friends, and disfavoring his opponents, led him to prostitute the vast and growing patronage of the general executive office to reward the services of all who had contributed to his individual or party success.

James Buchanan, whose aid had, perhaps, availed to turn the doubtful presidential election in Jackson's favor, and who, to accomplish this, had perfidiously turned against his bosom friend and former patron, the opposing candidate, was unblushingly invited to reward himself with the honors and emoluments of a choice embassy. The present chief justice of the Supreme Court, as before remarked, was given this place as a reward for services of doubtful legality, which his more honorable predecessor in the secretary-ship of the treasury would not sell himself to perform. The ablest graduates of the naval and military academies were compelled to resign, or take rank under idle, worthless boys, and used-up politicians, whose only claim on prefer-ment was, that they or their friends had contrib-uted to the success of the Jackson party.

The result was, a powerful political organiza-tion, having for its ruling principle the acquisi-tion and retaining of office for the sake of its patronage, and this patronage to be distributed as the reward of party services.

XXIX.

THE scantiness of the public revenue, and the pressure of the public debt, had till now enforced a frugality that had kept the offices of the general government eminently clear of the herd of cormorants, that, like carrion crows about a putrid carcass, persist in cursing with their pestiferous presence the government whose abundant resources are fitted to gratify their insatiate and undiscriminating appetites. The consequence was that ability and faithfulness to public trust were the practical and recognized passports to not over-paying offices. But now, a plethoric treasury, ample resources, a practically extinguished national debt, the vast and increasing number of public functionaries, called for by the rapidly-increasing area of settled territory, all contributed to render the period of Jackson's administration preëminently tempting for the ingress of a plundering horde to the multiplied, and still multiplying subordinate offices in the gift of the chief executive.

To this peculiarity of the times, add the peculiarity of President Jackson's personal character as put forth in the aphorism which he unblushingly established as a ruling law in respect to political contestants,—" To the victors belong the spoils," — and we have only to attribute to the community around him an ordinary amount of corruptibility, in order to predicate of his political adherents, and of his and their successors, qualifications for office and deportment in office, exactly the reverse of what characterized their predecessors.

From this time forward, the grand aim and study of every political man necessarily became, first, the art of controlling voters; and second, the art of counteracting the efforts of rivals similarly employed.

Perhaps the purgatorial fires of the present war, and the enormous incumbrance of the resulting war-debt, are the easiest, and the only agencies capable of reversing the prevalent prostitutions of political functions, that have been induced under the late succession of so-called Democratic administrations.

A galaxy of preëminently able statesmen, who defended the national interests at that time, coerced the administration into some decent regard for appearances. This induced concealment of those corruptions which would otherwise have shocked the moral sense of a hitherto comparatively virtuous people; * and, it also led to the deeper and more thorough planting of the principles to which the then prevalent party owed its strength; so that a longer time was secured for the germinating of those principles, and the people were gradually and insensibly accustomed to practices of political fraud from which they would otherwise have strongly revolted.

Those statesmen were occupied in defending the Constitution and the first principles of the government, from assaults that came thick and fast upon them, under the august profession of the policy of the administration; while in fact said assaults were really a blind, to divert attention from what was really the policy of the administration, namely, the prostituting of all the powers of government to party purposes,— to the emolument and immunity of that line of succession which was to be filled with the most active and least-principled individuals who should rise to the surface in that polluted caldron, the so-called Democratic organization.

---

*Not far from the close of Jackson's administration, the buildings of both the Post Office and Treasury Departments were destroyed by fire. And as one or both were fire-proof buildings, and much of the evidence of fraudulent governmental dealing was commonly known in the vicinity, little doubt was entertained by citizens residing thereabout, that the fires were set intentionally on the inside, to destroy the record of such dealing.

Had this principle been discerned and demonstrated in the first place, and held up before the public gaze till the last, to the exclusion of all other issues, its disastrous operation might, perhaps, to some extent, have been averted. But the fatal error of the able men who defended the Constitution and the interests of the country, was, to join issue with their opponents upon various political questions, and argue their time, breath, and power, away on these, while the real source of danger was almost undiscerned and unresisted; and, as for the particular political questions argued, the so-called Democratic leaders would adopt or abandon any and all of them as best suited their one ruling aim. Perhaps with the increasing resources and necessarily increasing expenditures of the government, an air of lavish looseness would have crept in, under an executive of the most frugal principles. But to anticipate the coming change from poverty to affluence, to obtain the reins of government at this particular juncture, and so dispose of all the patronage at command, both legitimate and factitious, as to lay the foundations deep and broad for perpetuating power in that particular party, by systematic corruption,—this was the function of the Locofoco, or so-called Democratic, organization, and displays its inimitable genius.

XXX.

UNDER the administration of General Jackson, during two successive terms of four years each, followed immediately by that of Van Buren, the Vice-president of his second term and the successor of his choice, whose avowed ambition it was to " follow in the footsteps of his illustrious predecessor," the characteristic principle and policy of the party of which these two men may with propriety be said to have been the founders, became confirmed and influential beyond the reach of permanent and successful resistance. Some of the details of its operation require to be examined.

First : its effects upon the political periodical press were such as to command the devotion at first of a large and influential number, and eventually, of a large majority, of the newspapers, which were almost the only source of political information for the people, especially in the older of the Northern States. This devotion was evinced by such a universal and persistent suppression of whatever was damaging, such a magnificent presentation of whatever was favorable to the party, such a warping and falsification of current history, that a discriminating and disinterested foreigner, attached to one of the legations at Washington, on inquiring of one of Van Buren's friends for the best journal of their party, felt himself compelled to reject everything that could be brought forward, as unfit to be read by any fair-minded man. It was the policy of the leaders of this party, to keep it as isolated and distinct as possible. Its voters were, as far as practicable, inspired with feelings of animosity toward all political opponents, and with feelings of intolerance for any version of facts, other than such as emanated from their own party press. Under these circumstances, the operation of such a party periodical literature could not be difficult to predict. It must put an enormous despotic power into the hands of those who, by controlling the patronage of the general government, dictated the utterances of that party press. It must have educated, and it did educate, the common voters of that party, unquestioningly and unwaveringly, to submit to whatever of dictation came to them through their recognized party leaders. These leaders they were induced to regard as the only true and trusty patriots and statesmen, while all

besides were fools and knaves. THEIR LOVE OF
COUNTRY WAS THUS TRANSMUTED INTO LOVE OF PARTY,
and many of them were brought sincerely to
believe that the sum of all impending public
calamities would inevitably follow the transfer
of the treasury keys to other than the hands of
their own party magnates. The editors of these
partisan journals were led to expect, and, for the
most part, were eventually made to experience,
that it was not unprofitable to serve their political masters.

At the South, and in portions of the Western
States, where the common people were less educated, less was done by the press, and more by
popular orators. These were indoctrinated, and
toned by their chiefs, and made in their several localities to perform the functions elsewhere assigned to a subsidized and unprincipled press.

Second: in pursuance of the same general
party policy, and by the application of similar
instrumentalities, the foreign-born population
were taken hold on, and their political influence
secured to a cause about which they knew nothing, but that its adherents flattered their prejudices, pandered to their vices, talked more loudly
in favor of licentious freedom, and dealt out to
them more of the dictation to which they had

15

been accustomed in their native monarchies, than anybody else presumed to do.

Third: the terms Democracy and Democratic were made, with some success, to play a magnificent part in covering up and denying the real attitude and aims of the fraternity; while the general plan was adopted of bringing into the connection not only the foreign-born, but *all the lower, less intelligent, more vicious, blind, and violent portions of the whole population, and of arraying them in hostile prejudice against the more principled, intelligent, and discreet,* dubbing the latter as aristocrats.

The plan of appropriating the United States revenues as a reward for party services operated with such effect that the party often found itself in such undisputed power as to be able to resort to some obviously iniquitous and injurious displays of power, for the purpose of driving from its ranks the more intelligent and conscientious portion of the people, of bringing upon itself such opposition as would serve as a pretext for inspiring its own blind adherents with increased degrees of party violence and hate, and thus widening the difference, and aggravating the hostility that prevailed between those who were within and those who were without the boundaries of this party organization. This made the position of their own office-holding, office-seeking, adherents more obviously distinct and desperate, and had the effect of obtaining from them more desperate and persevering exertions to perform their assigned part of carrying the elections.

Fourth : applying improved modes of carrying important elections became an important branch of occupation for the ablest minds in the fraternity. Executive abilities of the highest order were called into exercise in this department. The subordination of parts was rendered as complete almost as in a military organization. Writing and speaking abilities of the highest order were employed and paid for. A fixed per centage on their salaries was regularly exacted from those who enjoyed the gift of salaried offices in the services of the government; contracts for government supplies and services were so managed as to yield immense sums for party purposes, and when these sources of supply were insufficient, magnificent defalcations were now and then resorted to.

Such was the state of self-control and discipline, throughout the party, that a sublime reticence sometimes marked the incubation of their most desperate and decisive operations.

The surveying of the whole field of contest, and the husbanding of resources, so as to neglect

all those parts where their own party was so
strong as to make success certain without effort,
and also those parts where the opposition was
so strong as to render effort hopeless, and centre
all available influences on those few fulcral
points where defeat would be fatal to the party
sustaining it, is one of the highest attainments
that had been advanced to, by this colossal combination of perverted governmental powers,
prostituted to the perpetuation of power in a
corrupt political party organization.

It is in violent struggles to carry such limited
localities which exert a decisive influence on
extensive elections, that fraud, perjury, and corrupt practices were more frequently resorted to.

At a certain time, not far from the close of
General Jackson's second official term, while the
administration party and their opponents were
very nearly balanced in the lower house, the
seat of a member from Pennsylvania fell vacant,
perhaps by death. An election was held to fill
that vacancy. It was of very great importance
to the administration party to carry that election.
The people of Pennsylvania, despite the falsifica-
tions of the party press and speakers, knew
themselves to have been damaged to the extent
of many millions of dollars by recent acts of the
executive, in depriving their iron works of the

benefit of a protective tariff, and in destroying the United States Bank, which had always been in their chief city. Hence it was known that the vote in the vacant district would be heavily against the administration.

John B. Clark, at that time a carriage-maker of Gettysburg, Pa., an active politician of the administration party, — who afterwards removed to southern Missouri, was there elected to Congress for two or three successive terms, took a prominent part in defeating the election of Sherman of Ohio to the speakership of the second Congress of Buchanan's term, and was afterward expelled from the House for being in arms against the government at the battle of Boonville, — took an active part in carrying the election to fill the above-named vacancy in Pa., of which, some years afterwards, he gave the present writer the following account : " We imported voters from Baltimore, New York, and Quebec ; some of them we boarded on expense for weeks, or perhaps months, before the election. Some of the smartest of them voted four times in one day, and perjured themselves every time, and we paid them for it." Clark also went on to describe the process by which the State elections were systematically controlled by party leaders of the same dye, and the expenses of the opera-

15*

tion defrayed from the profits of a preconcerted plan of colluding to plunder the public treasury.

A volume might be filled with authentic accounts of similar transactions, (perhaps instead of a volume I should have said a library,) but this must suffice as a specimen.*

While such transactions were being carried on, the administration press was hurling such a storm of abuse and vilification on their opponents as to lead disinterested persons to suppose that whatever of the above and like historic truth was uttered by those opponents was so uttered under the excitement of irritated feeling, and to repel assault.

* See Appendix E.

XXXI.

THE common masses of a political party, thus combined and dealt with, must of necessity be rapidly preparing to become the instrument of anything its leaders see fit to employ it about; whether the enterprise be the consummation of some gigantic treason against the government, or whether it be the more quiet and protracted process of controlling the elections and appropriating the public revenues for the benefit of their party leaders. But the effects which such a party organization, so combined and controlled, must produce, beyond the boundaries of its own enclosure, deserve examination.

That portion of the community who least appreciate the sacredness or worth of the elective franchise, together with those of more intelligence who are least disposed to see that franchise guarded and preserved, constitute the combination, which, from its preëminent strength and efficiency, as well as from its being the first

of its kind, deserves to be designated *the party*.
Those who are outside the boundaries of this
party organization suddenly find themselves excluded from almost all voice and participation in
the affairs of government. The limits which
patriotism, self-respect, common justice, and fair
dealing have hitherto set to party violence and
usurpation have been spurned and disregarded
by their opponents. By means before unheard-
of and unsuspected, the casual majority of the
hour HAVE CHANGED THEIR TRANSIENT ASCENDENCY
INTO A PERMANENT USURPATION OF THE REINS OF
GOVERNMENT; and those who are left outside of
the usurping party have nothing left for them
to do but to pay taxes. Their only alternative
is, to organize and attempt to operate a rival
party. This they attempt to do.

But they are not equal to their teachers at
organizing. They have no such pliant mass to
act on, no taste or disposition to act the tyrant
and the demagogue over it if they had. Dec-
ades of peace and affluence have banished fear
and nursed presumption in the popular mind
respecting national security; and patriotism has
almost died out for lack of exercise. The public press and public speakers have been so far
suborned that it is next to impossible to make
any extensive impression on the public mind

respecting the existing state of things or the future prospect. No argument that can be educed can counteract among the masses the influence of interested leaders, bent on the attainment of office by the exercise of party zeal. Falsehood and vituperation are used by the dominant party to the wildest extent, and with the effect to create an impression of more or less general extent *that their opponents lie as badly as they do themselves, and are as dishonest and corrupt.* This general impression that all political men are corrupt, and that all their utterances, being designed for party ends, are as likely to be false as true, seems to cut off the last channel through which any effort can be directed to retrieve the general demoralization and despotizing of the popular masses. The intelligent and patriotic seem doomed to sit down helpless, and see the dreadful work go on, till the madness becomes so excessive as to produce a reaction and correct itself. Twice did the evil run to this extent, and twice did this corrective reaction take place, and the dominant party in 1840 and in 1848 simply through the excess of its obviously corrupt maladministration was defeated in its attempts to elect its party candidate to the presidency. And twice did a very singular interposition of divine Providence, or some assassinating

instrument of human designing, cut suddenly
short the lives of the men who were elected to
the chief magistracy contrary to the wish and
purpose of the leaders of the otherwise invariably successful party. Thus leaving that party a
practically unbroken series of successes from the
inaugurating of General Jackson, in 1828, to
1860, when its leaders, assembled in convention
at Charleston for traitorous purposes, elected to
defeat themselves; and, as a consequence, in the
following year Abraham Lincoln was called on
to do the best he could in an effort to gather up
and reunite the palsied and putrescent fragments of a severed Union.

In the mean time, the portion of the people
who had been left out in the formation and continuance of the dominant party, seeing the
worse than uselessness of attempting to operate a rival party organization, abandoned the effort. The more able and discriminating of them
retired from concern in public affairs. The
more corruptible of them at last joined the
dominant party, or, in combination with such as
occasionally fell off from that party organization, on principles more or less allied to those
of the old parent, formed the succession of nascent, imperfect, and shortlived party organisms
which have successively borne the honor of be-

ing the opposition, since the Whigs disbanded, one of which caught the crumbling government and happened to have the national administration fall into its hands when, at the close of Buchanan's term, the party that elected him, true to its principles, mature in its tendencies, with traitorous intent, achieved its suicide.

XXXII.

THE PROSTRATION RESULTING TO A PATRIOTIC MINORITY, FROM THE USURPATION OF A DESPOTIC FEW, CONTROLLING A MAJORITY.

In case of hopeless and unendurable abuse of power, under a monarchical government, armed rebellion affords a natural, and at least temporarily successful, method of redress. As long as the monarchical form of government is continued, it can hardly be said to be a revolution for a people inured to being dictated to, to change one master for another. But in a democracy, revolution, when once begun, tends strongly to become chronic. Besides this, when the majority of the voters can be irredeemably cajoled by a succession of graceless villains, whose vocation it is to manage voters for their own and their party's benefit, the last of human remedies appears to have been exhausted. With such a cajoled or cajolable majority, a revolution — unless it be a revolution back to despotism — can accomplish nothing, unless it be, if possible, a nearer approach to anarchy, or a chronic condition of revolt and intestine war.

Under this condition of affairs, the prevalent practical course with us has been, for men of patriotism and ability to abandon politics and all practical concern in governmental matters, and to devote themselves to private business and personal and family aggrandizement, in other lines of action; consoling themselves with the reflection that the people rule, and have everything their own way.

It may seem hard to say that more than this is required of a democratic member of a democratic community. Yet the events of the current crisis compel us to admit, and to act on the admission, that much more is required; even the temporary resigning of almost every personal right, and the submitting of ourselves to military discipline, with the certainty of experiencing very great hardships, privations, and sufferings, with the imminent risk of losing health, limb, and life itself. What is the conclusion? This, namely, if the privilege of existence as a democratic member of a democratic community is liable to cost all this, in a crisis that imperils the nation's life, it is reasonable, and no more than reasonable, that, to avert the occurrence of such a crisis, something more should be done than merely to submit to the majority, and then, besides this passive duty, turn one's entire atten-

tion, concern, and effort to the work of personal
and family aggrandizement. *The efforts of designing demagogues should be counteracted with a
liberal portion of the persistency, the zeal, the personal hazard and the cost, with which, when the crisis
arrives, we are obliged to contend for national existence on the tented field, and in the battle's strife.*
The inadequacy of public legislation, the maladministration of public officers, the deliberate
frauds and falsehoods of partisan . politicians,
combinations to defeat the ends of justice and
the achieving of the public weal, should be uncovered and explained by men who are known
to have higher ends in view than to fatten at
the public crib.

It were better that the code duello, with all
its evils, should prevail than that millions of
voters in our democratic government should be
fed by the half century together on nothing but
the political fiction and falsehood which designing knaves, who are incapable of any higher
aim than to plunder the public treasury for personal and party benefit, see fit to deal out to
them, till another war like the present, with the
slaughter of its tens of thousands shall result.

Perhaps no other operating cause, but the
throes of expiring despotism, could have produced such a colossal and infuriate combination

as is now struggling to overthrow democracy in this country. But *had those on whom it devolved to sustain democracy in this country for the past quarter of a century, been more persistent and inquiring, and less presuming, puerile, and supine, the disaster which the country is now suffering could never have occurred.* It may be true that no motive *cause* but the throes of expiring despotism could have induced the present assault on the life of our nation: but it is also true that without the powerful collateral aid of a despotic and traitorous party of Northern citizens to assist them. the Southern despots who are now threatening our capitol and invading the Free States with an army of a hundred thousand men. could scarcely have survived the first year of their onslaught.

One of the most extensively disastrous effects produced outside of its own limits. by the party on whose chronicle we are dwelling. was the obliterating of the public conscience and the thorough spread of corrupt principles and practices in respect to everything political: so that material impressed with political honesty can hardly be found. wherewith to constitute a ruling majority. even when the despotized fraternity which has ruled the country for the past thirty years shall have been displaced.

How far the presumptuous supineness and pue-
rility of our Northern statesmen are legitimate
results of the rich and hitherto almost costless
immunities conferred by our system of free government, and to what extent they are justly at-
tributable to the governmentless mythologies
which obtain among us so extensively in the
religious world, are questions that may be sug-
gested here, but which it lies not within the
assigned limits of these pages to discuss.

When it comes to be the unmistakable testimony of current history, that there is not force
enough in our national administration to punish
the most flagrant malfeasance in office, or the
most gigantic frauds, it is the opinion of the
present writer that a little judicious blood-letting, after the manner of William Tell, would be
for the public health. And that when this or
other remedial action is deferred to the all-absorbing vocation of personal and family aggrandizement, there exists a festering plethora which
betokens disastrous sickness of the civil system.
It is a sign of unhealthiness in the system, when
the powerlessness of public justice can be calculated on only by the baldest villains. " It is "
sometimes " expedient that one man should die
for the people, that the whole nation perish
not."

XXXIII.

ANDREW JACKSON was not a Secessionist; Martin Van Buren was not a Secessionist. How, then, came it to pass that the party, of which these men were the founders and fashioners, should become a powerful and efficient instrument in the hands of Jefferson Davis and his coadjutors for destroying the United States government?

Jackson, Van Buren, their compeers and successors of the same political school, down to James Buchanan, did one thing; namely, they combined, kept up, and operated, a political party on the following principles: among the membership, unqualified devotion to *the party* and unquestioning obedience to its leaders, with unscrupulous and vindictive hostility to every one who opposed them; among the leaders, the usurpation of the government, for the sake of its honors and emoluments, to be appropriated, first, to perpetuate the usurpation, and, second, to aggrandize themselves individually.

Patriotism and justice, veracity and self-respect,

in short, every sentiment more elevated or sacred than the honor proverbial among thieves, was effectually replaced by a blind, unscrupulous devotion to performing the dictates of party leaders. Instead of fearing for the destruction of their country, and instead of being purposed, at all costs, to avert any detriment or disaster that might threaten the precious civil institutions which their fathers bequeathed, and to which they owed their unparalleled prosperity, the damnable political demagogues who assembled at the national capitol, under guise of executive administration and legislature, had brought the popular masses of their party to a state of mind in which they feared *nothing* but the defeat of their party candidate, no matter who he might be, and were perfectly purposed at every cost to defend *nothing* but the succession of miscreants, who should be designated in secret party conclave to succeed each other, in wielding the usurped governmental powers for party purposes, and in disposing of the public treasure for personal aggrandizement, — a state of mind in which they could see nothing offensive but the real or imaginary faults of political men who belonged not to their party, nothing to be feared but the exposure, breaking up, and reform of that deep and dark and long-continued series of atrocities, into supporting and defending which themselves had been betrayed. To avert these feared results, no sacrifice was too costly, no application too assiduous.

James Buchanan and Isaac Toucey, two despicable lickspittles of the perjured crew who ruled over them, and used them and their official power to initiate the present dreadfully disastrous War, are but mature and ripe specimens of what the principles and practices of their long dominant party have tended, more or less effectually, to make of every Northern man, who, for the last thirty years, has consented to be counted in its numbers.

The results, to the Union, of the official conduct of James Buchanan and Isaac Toucey,— the deliberate giving up of the army and navy, the forts and arsenals of the country, into the hands of conspirators leagued to destroy the government,— are nothing more nor less than the results which the principles and practices of their party have directly, and more or less effectually, tended to produce, ever since that party first received its characteristic impress from the consecutive administrations of Andrew Jackson and Martin Van Buren. The truth of this remark is amply attested by the pertinacity with which — notwithstanding the defection of such men as Butler, and Corcoran, Busteed, D. Dickinson, Shepley of Maine, McClernand of Indiana, and hundreds more of the ablest and most honest that ever were caught in the meshes of a colossal, corrupt, and traitorous party organization — the major part of the masses of that party, up to the fall elections of 1863, under the lead of C. L. Vallandigham, Fernando Wood, and Horatio Seymour, still adhere to the cause of their old Southern leaders.[*]

The Southern oligarchy under Jefferson Davis conspired to overthrow the government, that they might obtain a large fragment from its ruins whereon to erect an empire sacred to despotism in general and to African slavery in particular, from whence to fulminate destruction on all antagonists, to the boundaries of the continent, and to the end of time.

It will be seen that there is no very positive contrariety between the aims of the two fraternities. Up to the time at which the Southern conspiracy matured into armed treason, nothing was necessary but for the conspiring party to conceal their ulterior design, and the two fraternities were one in spirit and in action, straining every nerve to beat down their common opponents. Up to this point, the only difference be-

* See Appendix F.

tween the two affiliated parties was, that the Southern wing would and the Northern wing would not prosecute their common vocation to the point of armed rebellion.

But the same qualities which had given Southern men a ruling ascendency in the government of the nation had, nearly or quite from its origin, given them a ruling ascendency in the Jackson-Buchanan party. This ascendency they had used to impart to their subalterns and partisans, particularly at the North, a party spirit of the utmost virulence, and habits of party action to the last degree violative of the dictates of honor, honesty, justice, and patriotism. So that, up to the time at which these Southern leaders of the party threw off all disguise and assumed the attitude of armed rebellion, their Northern coadjutors, President Buchanan among the foremost of them, were ready and earnest to engage in anything, no matter how dishonorable, unjust, mendacious, or treasonable, so long as it did not expose their own necks to the halter, and they could be shown some plausible reason to believe that the proposed measure would result to the benefit of their political party. Hence the dispersion of the United States army and navy, the rifling of the arsenals and treasury, and the almost utterly defenceless exposure of the

Southern forts, mint, and shipyards, preparatory to opening the present hostilities, which preparation James Buchanan assisted in accomplishing, and his Northern adherents assented to, for the benefit of their political party, and in obedience to their political leaders.

At the time of the attempted execution of the nullification project, this school of treason, of which the present seceding body is the outgrowth, was confined to South Carolina. The issue on which this project worked was the tariff. The effort was to unite the South in resistance to the government on the ground, as was pretended, that the general government, under the influence of Northern men, would tax Southern imports for the sake of protecting Northern manufactories.

Upon the suppression of this conspiracy, by the prompt energy of President Jackson, it is matter of history that the defeated leaders of that scheme took counsel, and determined to change the issue from the tariff to the slavery question, assured that the whole South could be united on this latter issue, and on nothing else. The doctrine of State sovereignty, or the superiority of State authority over the authority of the general government, was from this time propagated with the utmost industry, especially at the

South, for the poisoning of the popular mind, and to prepare a foundation upon which, at the proper time, the Secession edifice could be reared. From this time, also, no doubt, it was that the clique of traitors who remodelled their plans after the failure of their South Carolina nullification, saw the important benefit which would result to them by having a general political party under their control, selected the Jackson-Buchanan party as best suited to answer their ends, gathered themselves into it as honest *bona fide* members, took it under their control, and began to manage it for the accomplishment of their own purposes.

When, after the death of President Taylor, and the defeat of the Whigs in attempting to elect his immediate successor, the Whig party gave up its organization and became practically extinct, these Southern leaders of the Jackson-Buchanan party, by preventing either the re-formation of the Whig or the successful organization of any other opposition party in the Southern States, achieved this important result; namely, that the opposition which was raised against them, if it ever assumed a party form and organization, must of necessity be a sectional party, confined to the Northern States. This result they found themselves able to accomplish by virtue of the despotic control they already possessed over the non-slave-holding population of the Southern States.

So remote were the Northern people from anything like ostensible monarchy, that the dictation of this clique of despots came to them like the " Vox populi, vox Dei," by which the Democrat is always governed. And when they cried against Abraham Lincoln and his supporters, " Black Republican," " Abolitionist," the latter seemed to shrink back and shudder, as if they had been rebuked by a voice from heaven. Whereas, the seven and three-fourths millions of non-slave-holding whites in the South had scarcely more to do with originating or reiterating this outcry, or with inducing the sectionalized state of the anti-despotic party, than had the black slaves that served under the same masters.

XXXIV.

RECAPITULATION OF THE PART PERFORMED BY THE JACK-
SON-BUCHANAN PARTY IN BRINGING ABOUT THE PRESENT
WAR.

ON this branch of our general subject we re-
sume as follows: — The disposition and power
for despotic usurpation was produced and nourished into strength in this Republic, by having
an abject mass of Africans consigned to perpetual bondage by the laws and Constitution of the
country as commonly interpreted.

This disposition and power for despotic usurpation first manifested itself in the form of
overt treason, in South Carolina, during the administration of President Jackson, in an attempt
to nullify the laws of Congress by authority of
the individual State. This attempted treason
against his government was promptly suppressed
by Jackson; who also founded a political party,
which, without literally infracting the Constitution, usurped, and, with the exception of two
brief and partial interruptions, for thirty years,
held the United States government for its own
use and behoof; and this it succeeded in accom-

plishing by virtue of distributing the government revenues as plunder to be divided out in reward for party services.

This usurping party, though distributed through the Northern as well as through the Southern States, like the general government, was under the practical and permanent control of leading Southerners. At least they soon placed themselves in such control.

As the natural tendencies to despotic usurpation developed in these leading Southerners, and as the necessities of their situation pressed them more and more, they formed the intelligent design to break up the government, and on a portion of its ruins found an empire for themselves, free from the embarrassing presence of a democratic people and democratic institutions. Next to this in point of time came the purpose of using the party which Jackson founded, to demoralize and divide the North; at the same time extinguishing all organized opposition in the Southern States. They did much to conceal their real aim, by successfully monopolizing to themselves and to their adherents the political appellatives " Democrats" and " Democracy." They despotized and depraved their own party in the North, by accustoming them to march under training file-leaders, as

near upon the verge of treason as they could
go and not precipitate war. They demoralized
that portion of the Northern people whom they
could not control, by rendering political integrity useless, and perfidious corruption practically unobjectionable.

When they had matured their arrangements
and completed preliminary operations in these
several directions, having also disposed of the
treasury, army, navy, arms, and military stores
of government to their satisfaction, they then
deliberately broke up their own political party,
thereby throwing the responsibilities of the dis-
mantled government into the green hands of an
ill-connected sectional minority, opened their
overwhelming batteries on Fort Sumter, and
advanced their legions by rail to beleaguer
Washington.

The elements of success had hardly been miscalculated on the part of the traitors. Their
sway over the Southern masses was absolute
and unconditional, while the whole North did
not contain a man in whom any considerable
portion of the people felt that they could con-
fide the conduct of public affairs in the crisis
that was forced on them; there was scarcely
known to be a military officer who could credi-
tably handle an army of ten thousand men;

there was a natural certainty that the best of
such officers as should be called out by the
emergency would be sacrificed to the jealousy
of rival aspirants; the habits and character of
the Northern people were as remote as possible from warlike pursuits; the interruption of
their gainful industry would double to them the
calamities of every campaign, irrespective of
victory or defeat; it would be a slow and difficult process to inspire such a people with anything like martial spirit or enthusiasm; the
conspirators had a political party more or less
reliably attached to them interspersed throughout the North, with powerful influence to menace the administration and counteract its efforts,
and ready to act as spies on every square mile
of Northern territory, in every regiment of soldiers, in many important positions of civil and
military trust, in either house of Congress, in
every executive department, and not improba-
bly, in the very bed-chamber of the Chief Magistrate;* the noted honesty and mildness of
Mr. Lincoln would give the conspirators extensive immunity in traitorous crime and violence,
and the powerful prestige that pertains to a
bold, decided, severe, unrelenting course of ac-

---

* No suspicion is here intended to be thrown on any member of President Lincoln's family.

tion ; and last, but not least, the inexperience of those into whose hands the government must be intrusted would be a source of certain and extensive feebleness. The only points in which the conspirators appear to have miscalculated, were two : the unreliability of their own corrupted partisans in the North, and the exhaustlessness of the recuperative energies of a truly democratic people.

In respect to the former of these two points, the work of converting back the masses of a great political party from democracy to despotism must have been very imperfectly performed, being undertaken and carried on in the midst of the most democratic community on earth. There were multitudes of men in the ranks of that party who would tread the verge of treason to secure a party victory, while under the influence of heated party feeling, and excited by the presence of active leaders incessantly laboring to deceive them, who would still refuse to make the damning plunge across that boundary, merely to save the necks of their absent masters. The very injury that had been done to their better principles might naturally enough be expected at length to react against the villains by whom they had been instructed.

Respecting the recovering power of a true

democracy, the world has had but little experience, and the truth in this regard would of necessity be slow to reach the attention or secure the belief of a crew of half barbarous despots battling for the extinction of all democracy, until such time as they shall be privileged to read that important truth evinced in the fact of their own helpless overthrow.

XXXV.

No history of the causes that contributed to bring about the existing calamitous intestine war will be complete, which does not give a somewhat prominent consideration to the character and influence of the Abolitionists, technically so called. By this term I would be understood to describe a sect of political religionists who have made themselves conspicuous in the Northern States for the last thirty years, as the special advocates and champions of freedom and morality in their bearings on slavery in the Southern States.

The leaders of this sect, and of necessity its members to a great extent, are distinguished for a virulent rejection of the great truths of revealed religion, while yet they are the exceedingly zealous advocates of an indefinite and variable code of deistical morals, framed in part according to suggestions drawn from the same sacred Scriptures whose supreme authority they vehemently despise. The object of their deistical worship is usually represented by themselves as shorn of every lineament of vindictive justice, and endowed with imperturbable, illimitable, indiscriminate benevolence toward the members of the human family, irrespective of moral character, acts or aims.

Of course, in a religion like this, the holding of one's fellow-man in involuntary servitude would be the sin of sins. It would partake almost of the heinousness of beef-eating under the mythology of ancient Egypt. And the obvious infirmity of the deity of this modern sect would remain to be made up to a great extent by the zeal and activity of his worshippers.

We have elsewhere observed that the highly religious character of the early settlers of New England appears still in form to characterize their descendants, even when the latter have abandoned entirely the foundations on which their fathers reared the structure of their religious faith and practice. Among these, the Abolitionists hold a prominent place.

We have also elsewhere remarked, that after the adoption of the Federal Constitution, and the freeing of the slaves in the Northern States, while, under the influence of the rising cotton trade, political sentiment in the South was verging back upon despotism, the principles and practices of free government, " for better for worse," were having unobstructed course, and were working out their natural tendencies without impediment among the people of the Northern States.

Probably it never occurred to the people of these States that there was any such thing as excess in loving political liberty. And the world may well wonder that there has been so little ; that Agrarianism, and Fourierism, and Communism, and their kindred degenerations of legitimate popular liberty, have had so few followers, and have produced among us so small results ; that constitutional civil authority has been so generally respected, so entirely preserved, that it remained for the representatives and abettors of despotism to do the first acts that tended in any material extent to mar or undermine the goodly governmental structure which our republican ancestors bequeathed to us. But the class we are contemplating, deeming themselves happy in finding so prominent an object as Southern slavery, against which to vent their zeal, and a sentiment so universal, so deep-rooted, so blameless and unquestionable, as our inherited love of popular liberty, to which they could appeal for support and coöperation, soon made themselves the prominent leaders and champions of all who could be excited to pursue that liberty to excess.

The professedly Christian denominations who really denied the truth of the revealed Scriptures had by this time become numerous and influential. These had no objection to the Abolitionists on account of their infidelity; while very many members of evangelical churches felt their love of freedom so outraged by the fact of existing slavery and its attendant evils, that they forgot for a time their obligations of supreme allegiance to the authority of divine Revelation, and, with more or less sincerity, affiliated with those who derided a divinity who was not up to the times on the subject of human rights, and cursed alike the producers and the product of a civil Constitution which bound them to respect the rights of those who held their fellow-men in bondage.

Could the real character of the Abolitionists, and the real weight of their influence, have been known and admitted North and South, their due space in history would have been less than it now is. But circumstances peculiar to either section, and illy understood in the other, conspired to render their influence on the affairs of the country peculiarly infelicitous, and to some extent conducive to the present War.

Men brought up in the license of heathenism are kept quiet by its depressing ignorance, if not by the fetters of its superstition. But when one who has enjoyed the light and health-giving influence of revealed religion, and has been educated under more or less of its restraints, casts loose from its authority; as he begins to deal familiarly with things that other people reverence, and to spurn the boundaries which others never pass, in the estimation of undiscriminating multitudes, the noisy extravagance of his diction, and the unembarrassed celerity, the drunken freedom, of his mental gait are almost sure to be mistaken for superior intelligence, eloquence, and strength.

Thus it came about that the Abolitionists, who were really indefatigable in their labors, acquired a prominence before the public mind, and engrossed a share of attention, entirely disproportioned to either their political or moral strength.

So early and so effectually did they succeed in taking under their patronage the universal love of popular liberty in all its bearings on the enslaved, that it became practically impossible for any one, however true in his support of his country's Constitution, or however firm in his belief of the truths of revealed religion, to say or do anything tending to limit or withstand pro-slavery aggression without becoming more or less identified with these infidel leaders in the estimation of the observant but uncommitted public, particularly at the South.

XXXVI.

AMONG the first requisites of permanent popular liberty are popular self-restraint, implicit submission to constituted authorities, a sacred regard for the rights of the minority. In the Northern States, where popular liberty obtains in its greatest perfection, this, as well as every other requisite of that liberty is, and has long been, largely possessed. It was this popular self-restraint, this sacred regard for the rights of the minority, that secured immunity to the Abolitionists, while they ranted and blazed against the God of revelation, and the Constitution, and founders of the government.

At the South, where popular liberty never did prevail to any great extent, this popular self-restraint not only did not exist, but the very conception of such a thing was wanting. If any minority there offended against the sentiments and wishes of the majority, or of their political leaders, it was "mob them," "lynch them," "call a meeting, appoint a vigilance

committee," " tar and feather them," " duck
them," " cowhide them," " shoot them," " hang
them," — such was the verdict, and such the
execution, and not unfrequently the execution
came first. The Southern people knew of no
motive but cowardice or pusillanimity that could
prompt to a different course. When they became aware of the conduct of the Abolitionists
at the North, and also that they were not seriously interfered with, they of course concluded
that the majority of the Northern people were
of the same way of thinking, or too cowardly
and pusillanimous to resist. If some of the
more intelligent Southerners ascertained that
these views which they took of the people of
the North were not correct, they lacked both
the ability and disposition to disabuse the public
mind.

The Abolitionists were regarded at the North
as a set of harmless fanatics, who made a great
deal of noise, but exerted very little influence,
and produced no direct practical results, and
would ultimately sink of their own weight if let
alone. The divine declaration, " They that honor
me I will honor, and they that despise me shall
be lightly esteemed," has seldom been more obviously or more conspicuously fulfilled, than in
the history of this class of persons.

As much of the real anti-slavery sentiment of the Revolutionary period as survived in the South was early embodied in the Colonization Society, an association which aimed at and accomplished a great work for the negroes by withstanding the African slave-trade, by supplying a channel in which whatever of anti-slavery feeling existed in the South could exert itself, by demonstrating the capability of the negro race for improvement, civilization, and self-government, and by affording the masters who were disposed to emancipate their slaves an opportunity to do so with the prospect of the negroes being benefited by their freedom. This society was among the first recipients of the virulent antipathy of the Abolitionists. Henry Clay, the ablest statesman of his age, a living martyr to his lack of sympathy with pro-slavery politicians, and a prominent champion of Colonization, was rejected and defeated in the presidential canvass of 1844 by the Abolitionists of New York, who, by their factious course, procured the election of James K. Polk, the annexation of Texas, the war with Mexico, and the addition of three other of the spacious States from the northern portion of that republic, to extend the area of slave territory. By their feeble impractical ultraism, the Abolitionists generated a powerful reactive influence in favor of the pro-slavery loco-focos, the only effective allies of Secession at the North. Farther than this the history of their political influence at the North appears to be a blank.

At the South, however, they were regarded with more sincere concern and dread. They were, to the Southern mind, the representative of all that Northern love of popular liberty which was dangerous to slavery, and was fast coming to be distasteful to the common sentiment as it verged back on despotism. They were, more or less openly, the avowed enemie of revealed religion and of the civil Constitution The mist that hung about the limits of thei numbers and their strength served to magnify both indefinitely. It is true that they generall assaulted slavery at a very respectful distance but no one could tell what they might no accomplish through the mails and by secre emissaries, toward exploding the magazine o which the quiet of the Slave States is admitte to repose. They had no respect for the right c property in slaves; and, from ignorance or ma ice, — to the imperilled Southerner it mattere little which, — they had no fear of a servile insu rection being induced, nor any dread of the u told calamities which such an event would brin

The South was full of persons who were n

consciously to blame for the existence of slavery
among them. It was more than full of those
who denied the right of Northern fanatics, of
any class, more especially of infidels and anarch-
ists, to visit upon their heads the sins of their
fathers, or even their own sins, by bringing on
them wantonly the fact or the fear of servile
insurrection. They regarded the Federal Constitution as guaranteeing to them the right of "life,
liberty, and the pursuit of happiness," — even
the liberty of holding negroes as slaves, and
the pursuit of happiness in working them at
discretion, without interference from without
the limits of their own slave section; and with
any one who construed that great document
differently they could naturally have but short
parleying. The peculiar democratic virtue of
that self-restraint — that respect for the rights
of the minority which led the Northern people
to harbor and protect incendiaries while assaulting the peace of the South — was a virtue
of which they had no comprehension. Neither
were Southern minds ever able to comprehend the peculiar innocence, or excellence, of
that mode of logic by which slavery was
denounced as a "sin" against the deistical
morals of a class of men who revile the sacred
Scriptures and their divine Author.

18*

The Abolitionists were, and necessarily must have been, a source of extreme, incessant irritation to the people of the South, and enabled the despotic pro-slavery leaders to accomplish what they desired, in dividing the two sections from each other, and in arraying the people of each in hostility against the other. Without this irritation, the extreme bitterness which has been manifested at the South, throughout the present contest, against the Northern people, never could have been generated. Without the universal obloquy which has been brought upon the cause of negro freedom, by its most prominent advocates, President Lincoln would never have been able to keep his constituency quiet for a year and eight months after the opening of the war before issuing his Proclamation of Emancipation.

It may not be inappropriate here to suggest the inquiry, whether the peculiar tenets of that no-government class, — of whom the Abolitionists form a conspicuous specimen, who begin by abolishing future punishment, then capital punishment, and proceed along down to the practical abolition of all punishment,—have not been the source of much of the extreme, misplaced, and sickening leniency with which the present national administration has been wont to absolve culprits of every class and dye upon the guaranty of their mere idle promise to do better? — whether former administrations have not been to some extent affected by the same putrescent moral paralysis? — and whether the same is not a threatening source of national decadence?

To those who believe in a moral government of the universe, it may not be without interest or profit to inquire, whether the present protracted and afflictive war has not been divinely sent on the Northern States to check and turn back the growth of this no-punishment, no-government deism, the offspring of protracted affluence and peace, which has already done much to undermine the foundations of our nation's moral strength.

XXXVII.

THE third and last great collateral topic that enters into the plan of the present work, is the part taken by monarchists abroad in bringing about the Secession of the Southern States, and sustaining the present intestine War.

As the time approached for the full formation of a popular government on this continent, the monarchies of Europe grew sickly and disturbed. It was as if a demand for increased popular rights and liberties had been infused into the popular masses by an unseen hand. In England, this popular longing after liberty burst forth in the days of Cromwell, and, after annulling for a time the prerogatives of the monarch, allowed their restoration, but circumscribed the sphere of their action with a resistless hand. From that time down to the recent revolution in Italy, every nation has been more or less agitated by the same upheaval of the masses, the same irrepressible demand for enlarged popular rights and liberties. The result has been, that parties have been produced, monarchist and liberal, not with very definite boundaries, or with exact intelligent aims, but with strong, insatiate longings for the preservation or modification of the old monarchical system. The nobility, the privileged classes, the very wealthy, and the very poor, usually adhere to royalty; while the middle classes incline to popular liberty. The conflict between these two parties comes to direct intelligent collision only on sparse occasions. For the most part, it goes on in a dreamy, obscure manner, like the alternate dominance of disease and health, life and death, in the frame of a sufferer from severe disease. The antagonism is there; it is necessary, inevitable. The popular party has the irresolute, undetermined, unconscious strength; its antagonist has present possession of power, intelligent fear, and iron organization. It has learned much by experience in its protracted and deepening conflict. It has greatly modified its demands, its aims, and its modes of action. So much so that it seems almost to have combined within itself more or less of the constituent elements of its antagonistic principle, popular government. The reigns of Cromwell and of the Napoleon dynasty appear to be of a mongrel class, — a peaceful commingling of despotism and democracy. But all such specimens are transient, and soon subside to the one party or the other.

During the war of the American Revolution, while the real nature of democratic government, and its universal antagonism to monarchy, were not understood, moved by her chronic antipathy to England, France so far forgot herself as to take sides with the revolted colonies, and assist them to achieve their independence. This proved to be the first step toward the establishment of a system of democratic government, which has reacted disastrously on the cause of monarchy in the old world. By this act, France won the everlasting gratitude of the human family; but she planted in her own bosom the seeds of that popular commotion that ingulfed her ancient dynasty. No monarchy ever before had the opportunity, none since has had the fatuity, to commit such a blunder as to give willing aid to the natural enemy of all monarchies.

During the period in which only natural causes acted in converting the Southern people back from democracy to despotism, Europe was innocent of the change. When natural causes began to give place to intelligent design, it was otherwise.

No sooner did the idea enter a traitor's brain that something could be made by a severance of the American Union, than the desire, the expectation, the assurance of foreign aid came in to stimulate and confirm the traitorous intent. Not that the traitorous crew of Calhoun or of Davis understood, as we now understand, their own lapse back from democracy to despotism, or the necessary unanimity of all despotic hearts and hands, when their common interests are at stake, or the cause of popular freedom is to be assailed; but there was a felt bond of sympathetic union between the despot class in this country and their kind abroad.

These expectations of foreign aid were even greater than events have justified. Like the kindred expectations which were placed on their corrupted and enslaved political party in the North, these also were too sanguine. Not that the monarchical class in Europe were insincere or unfaithful, but their own situation was too delicate and critical; they lacked the power to do all that their hearts desired. The antagonism of their freedom-loving class in their own communities was too intense and threatening.*

* H. G. Moffat, a working man, thus speaks to the aristocratic sympathizers with the South in England, through the columns of the *Daily News:*

"It may be very fashionable with the upper ten thousand to sympathize with the slave-breeding aristocrats of the South, but we of humbler birth

The American despots judged the people of
Europe too much by the abject millions of their
own poor white population. The contempt they
had so often expressed for the headless populace
in the Northern States they began to think de-
served, and they transferred the same opinion
to the common mass, the liberty-loving class, in
Europe. These slaveholding despots had never
experienced the power of an intelligent, freedom-
loving people, undisciplined and unguided by a
monarchical head; and they were left, in their
intoxicated pride of power, to presume that
without monarchical guidance and headship
there could be no formidable strength. They
trusted to their own ability, by cutting off the
supply of cotton, to produce wide-spread distress, and they trusted to the mendacity of
themselves, and of their European friends, to interpret this distress to the public ear, as caused

have deeper ties that bind us to America, both political and social. When
we see the great number leaving our shores for that great country, and as
four out of six are relations of us common fellows, what will be our feelings? What of mine, having sisters and all that is very dear to me, if we
see our men-of-war bombarding New York City, knowing morally we have
been the cause? If we are not allowed to vote and make the government
here, we will not quietly allow the people's government to be destroyed
there. Working men are seldom heard in print upon this question; but let
not our gentry suppose there is no sympathy for the North here. They will
make an awful mistake if they go to war with America. It may be popular with the rich, the snobs and city swells, but not with working men.
Let them remember the Lancashire men starving first sooner than lift up a
finger against true liberty."— *Boston Journal, September 24th,* 1863.

by the belligerent movements of the United
States government, in case that government
presumed to move resistfully against the attempt
for its dismemberment.

They knew that there was, in foreign lands, a
strong antipathy toward this government; they
had themselves, while carrying on the government, experienced and taken pains to aggravate
this.* And the traitorous desire and purpose of
severing the States of the Union had no sooner
assumed an intelligent form, than fit and trusty
individuals of the monarchical class abroad began to be communicated with, consulted, and
confided in.

Not only were slave-holders at home and monarchists abroad united by a felt sympathy and
oneness of interest in their desire to assault and
ruin democracy wherever it presented itself,
but there was a kindred treason against the popular masses of their own communities, which in-

* Let it be remembered that, under the controlling influence of the same
traitorous heads that now control the Rebel Confederacy, the United States
government took a position of unfriendliness almost amounting to hostility
to England, when the latter power was engaged, with France, in the war
against Russia in the Crimea; and also that, under the same controlling influence, the proposal to abolish privateering, generally adopted in Europe,
was rejected by the United States government. And there appears at least
strong probability, if not proof, that in those and many like instances, unfriendliness to England on the part of our government was instigated by
those designing men on purpose to prepare England to pursue just such an
unfriendly course as she has pursued towards this government, in an
emergency like the present, which emergency was, by them, not unforeseen.

fluenced them severally alike. The slave-holding traitor had engaged to beguile and delude his seven and three-fourths millions of non-slave-holding white population into doing his fighting for him, at their own expense and at the imminent peril of their lives, and with the experience of all the disaster which unsuccessful warfare can inflict, and all, with no other prospect or reward, in case of success, but to complete and seal their own irreversible subjugation to their successful masters; while the European monarchist engaged to defraud and cajole the popular European masses into supporting him in his costly war alliance with the slave-holders, for the extinguishment of the spirit and institutions of popular freedom on this continent.

XXXVIII.

THE EXTENT AND EFFICIENCY OF EUROPEAN COÖPERATION WITH AMERICAN TREASON.

The natural sympathies, the interests, and leanings of the American slave-holders and the European monarchists being thus identical, it remains for history proper to present what evidence may reach the light concerning the time and manner, the terms and the extent, of obligations into which the latter entered to sustain the former in their efforts to break up this government.

It is already matter of history, that, almost upon receiving the first intelligence that armed traitors had assaulted the United States government, with a promptness and unanimity that demonstrate previous concert and collusion, the leading powers of Europe vouchsafed belligerent rights to the insurgents, thereby preparing the way for full recognition of their assumed nationality, menacing this government with that full recognition, and advancing as far toward it as they could and not incur a risk that amounts almost to a certainty of involving themselves in overt war, for breaking down the United States government, and for giving existence, strength, and character to the perfidious germ of a slave-holders' despotism.

While these governments were thus ingeniously approximating national alliance with the Southern traitors, in England particularly, the periodical press, as far as it could be controlled by the governing class, was set at work with all the infernal art and energy that money and mendacious malice could infuse, to inculpate and decry the government and people of this country, and to extol and sanctify the perjured crew who had undertaken to trample out this beacon light of liberty, and to erect their offshoot of Africa's barbaric despotism in its place.

This course was adapted and designed to discourage and weaken the loyal sentiment in the Northern States, to intimidate and depress the government, to embolden the northern allies of the Rebels; as far as possible to turn the opinion of the civilized world against us, and prepare the people of England and France to sustain their governments in farther steps in the direction they had started, if need should be, even to open war.

In England, the people had to be immediately appealed to and controlled, and the queen was as one of them. Their inclination to the side of freedom was strong, and their power to thwart the monarchical party was indisputable.

In France, there was nothing to be feared from the people, provided a general outbreak and domestic revolution were effectually guarded against; and, by imperial dictation, the empire was impoverished to send out and maintain an army of observation on the borders of this republic, ready to take advantage of the first opportunity for interfering, under the pretence of collecting a few millions of dollars, in bogus accounts, said to be due French subjects in Mexico.

It is matter of history, that the monarchical party in England succeeded so well as to be able to appropriate and spend between one and two millions sterling in equipping a fleet, and in sending troops to Canada, for war with the United States; and to have precipitated that war, had not our government, with more caution than boldness, averted the impending collision by releasing the captured emissaries of the rebels. England's dependence on the Northern States for grain to keep starvation from her borders served also to defeat the hankering of the monarchical party after war with the United States.

It is matter of history, that, while the British government confined itself to the line of a menacing and semi-hostile neutrality, members of the ruling class, in their individual capacity, did all that wealth, energy, and industry could do, with the connivance of the British government, and with no little success, to destroy American commerce on the seas, and, by running the blockade of Southern ports, to supply the Rebels with all the war material they needed.

In the early stages of the War, a curious smile must have passed over the countenances of these silent partners of the Rebel firm, on reading Secretary Seward's official predictions of the early closing of the War, founded as those predictions were on the Southern destitution of arms and war material; whereas they had themselves taken effectual measures to have this destitution supplied to satiety with the best arms, ammunition, and material which modern inventions, wealth, skill, and the workshops of Europe could produce.

It appears to have been in the campaign of our army in Mexico, during President Polk's administration, that the authors of the present rebellion, having effectually incorporated themselves with the Jackson-Buchanan party, suc-

ceeded in appropriating that political organization to their exclusive use. It was probably at
the Ostend Conference, held by our diplomats
in Europe during President Pierce's administration, that arrangements were perfected for in-
corporating the monarchists of Europe, as far as
possible, into the same combination.

Nothing but the blast of the breath of the
Almighty, sent forth for his own purposes, and
for his people's sake, is rendering this Confederation abortive.

The reigning powers of Europe (the Emperor
of Russia never was with them in their hostility
to this government) are not to be exactly identified with the monarchical class. The privileges and responsibilities of power, and considerations of state, served to modify the former,
and coerce them into a course of moderation
and hesitancy, with which the American traitors
had no sympathy at all, and their political allies
in Europe had scarcely more.

The concessions of our government, and the
demand for bread-stuffs from the Northern
States, deferred the consummation of active interference for our dismemberment, until at length
President Lincoln's adoption of the emancipation policy, tardy as it was, so stirred the love
of freedom in the minds of the European

masses that such interference became impracticable.

Thus the European allies of the traitor crew, next to their corrupted partisan supporters in the Northern States, failed them in their hour of need. And beyond the irritation, intimidating, and partial and transient, though repeated and frequent, embarrassment imposed on President Lincoln's government, and the protracting of the war and rendering it more exhausting to the North, and more entirely ruinous to the South, these allies have really contributed nothing to the success of the treason they undertook to aid.

XXXIX.

THE diabolical purposes of the European supporters of Secession in this country have found
a frequent and characteristic exercise in sending
across the ocean, at stated and well-timed intervals, a deluge of rumors and fabricated statements, complete and definite in circumstantial
detail, to the effect that France and England,
one or both, with, perhaps, other European powers, had determined, beyond reconsideration, to
enforce the separation called for by their admired
and loving partners in the South.   Hardly anything, during the course of the war, has been
more trying to the nerves of patriotic men, both
in and out of official station, than these repeated
and perpetual electro-infernal appliances.   Reason and facts disproved their claims to truth or
sanity; but, like some mysterious apparition,
that owes its disturbing power to its destitution
of substance, the possibility of a European combination to crush out democracy on this continent would, ever and anon, present itself, vast,

threatening, and obscure. Still farther to conjure down this boding apparition, and reduce this source of disturbing apprehension to its real substance and legitimate proportions, may well occupy the space of one or two intercurrent chapters that did not enter into the original purpose of this work. And these, while the printer is busy on other portions of the work, by the light of the New York riots, the success of the French in Mexico, and the confessions of a prominent Roman Catholic reviewer, we now attempt to supply.

The monarchical party in Europe, their deep and vital sympathy with Secession, their collusion, counsel, and coöperation with its managers, from its inception onward, we have before considered. But that the Roman Catholic church, "drunk with the blood of saints," and, from the heights of power which it once occupied, long since gone down under the universal execrations of all who were unblinded by its imbruting contact, should come forth, at this late day, and complicate itself with the confederate enemies of all civil freedom, was not, till recently, supposed to be practicable.

It is true that the debauched Northern partisans of the Southern despots have long been noticeably prompt and earnest to conciliate and

attach to themselves the foreign-born Romish
population. That the latter were numerous,
blind, passionate, and undivided, and, hence,
were eminently fitted to become stock in trade
for any unprincipled politician, was supposed to
be reason enough to explain the eagerness with
which they were sought. That the deep, dark
spirit of despotism in the presiding Southern
leaders of that party, drawn by the native sympathy of fellow-despots, fellows in guilt, was
yearning forth toward the papacy, like the
ascending toward the descending cone of a yet
unjoined waterspout, was not suspected, until,
in the hour of their greatest need, the papacy
in Europe, the papacy in Mexico, and the grovelling hell of the papacy in New York, struck
simultaneously for the rescue of the confederate
enemies of freedom.

Two hundred years ago, in Bedford jail, a
famous dreamer, whose dreams possess a definiteness and verity altogether surpassing the clear-
est vision of the most of waking observers, thus
described the papacy, under the figure of a
decrepit giant: "Though he be yet alive, he
is, by reason of age, and also of the many
shrewd brushes that he met with in his younger
days, grown so crazy and stiff in his joints that
he can do little more than sit in his cave's

mouth, grinning at pilgrims as they go by, and biting his nails because he cannot come at them."

A divinely-inspired writer, at a much earlier date, uncovering the then historic future of the world, presents the papacy in the form of " a beast having seven heads and ten horns, the body of a leopard, the feet of a bear, and the mouth of a lion ; and receiving his power, his seat, and great authority, from the dragon " that represented civil despotism ; from which dragon, also, the beast appears to have received the healing of a " deadly wound." Now no fact in modern history is more patent than that the papacy and civil despotism have long been leagued to support each other. So that it is not to be expected that one of these should receive a deadly wound, and the other would not writhe, and strive, as far as in its power, to heal its wounded partner. If Jeff. Davis & Co., the des-perate and determined champions of new-born despotism on this continent, after having ex-hausted the applications of the most unscrupu-lous military tyranny, to extort farther assistance from the impoverished, denuded, and devastated South, are being badly whipped, and on the point of hopeless overthrow before the advancing flushed, and stalwart armies of the North, noth-

ing is more natural, hardly anything more
necessary, than that the seven-headed beast, the
decrepit giant, should be in motion, to accomplish what is possible to be done for their
deliverance.

Hence we see that wily despot on the throne
of France, — who, in his Italian campaign, went
just far enough to receive the confidence of the
popular masses, far enough to gain the credit of
yielding to just so much of the pressure in favor
of popular freedom as it was past his power to
resist, far enough to humble a dangerous rival,
and to reduce the papacy to a position in which
it must know and feel that the continuance of
its existence was an imperial gift, — now in the
hour of greatest peril to the slave-holders' despotism, is found, by favor of the church of Rome,
establishing a military despotism in the city of
Mexico, and pouring along our Southern borders
a naval and military force limited by nothing
but his own discretion.

Simultaneously with this, evidently in obedience to orders issued from the Confederate capital, through the traitor leaders of the despotic *
party in the Northern States, New York City,
for successive days and nights, was committed
to the tender mercies of a Roman Catholic mob,

* See Appendix B, at the close of the volume.

20

describing which, an eminent literary writer,* who walked among them, hour after hour, uses the following language : "Tipsy women and boys (of whom the crowd was more than half composed) — the whole air and behavior of this wicked and dirty plurality expressed an exulting lawlessness and defiance — hives of sickness and vice. It is wonderful to see, and difficult to believe, that so much misery and disease and utter wretchedness could be huddled together, — lewd, but pale and sickly, young women, scarcely decent in their ragged attire, were impudent, and scattered everywhere in the crowd; numbers deformed, numbers made hideous by self-neglect and infirmity; numbers paralytics; drunkards, imbecile, or idiotic, forlorn in their poverty-stricken abandonment of the world — hideous, with hope and vanity all gone — the female form and features made frightful by sin, squalor, and debasement. There were no decent Irish among them. Irish they all were, — every one of them, — but they were the dirty, half-drunken, brutal rowdies. In ordinary life, such fellows sneak about and hide from daylight in places where they can drink and debauch and contrive wickedness; but here, where this grand fire made them feel like masters, and gave them

* N. P. Willis, of the *Home Journal.*

impudence for the hour, they were pictures of saucy beggars, half-drunken brutes, and robbers, longing to put a clutch upon your throat, and empty your pockets. One of our daily papers estimates this class of New York population at twenty thousand."

Outside the confines of the grossest heathenism, nothing but the debasing spiritual despotism of the Romish church has power to produce the subject for such a portraiture, — has power to prepare and furnish the instrument for such a desperate and dastardly assault on all that pertains to human well-being. It is the peculiar province and ability of that "mother of harlots" to reduce the worthiest races of the human family to a condition of depravity and vice and suffering wretchedness, and to endow them with dispositions of fiendish wantonness, to which not the savage state, the brute creation, nor hardly slavery itself, affords a parallel. Of all who have enjoyed the precious advantages of mature democracy, it is peculiar to the heart and habits of the despotized and traitorous Northern partisans of Southern despots, to order, and control, and put into active operation, the instrument which the papacy had provided for desolating the city of New York at the particular juncture when Lee, the military leader of the Confederate hosts, was invading Pennsylvania, Semmes, with his British cruisers, was burning American commerce at the mouths of Northern harbors, and the British press and ministry, with the subtle Frenchman joining in, were blowing their strongest, heartiest blast in favor of recognizing as real the assumed nationality and independence of the Confederate slaveocracy. This was also the point of time at which Napoleon III. first openly expressed himself possessed of the power and the will, by papal aid, to erect Mexico into a permanent despotism on our Southern border.

Read now a specimen of the style in which the papal priests and periodicals pronounce insidious curses on all that remains of civil freedom, and declare their admiration for the "gallant and noble" despots of the South who are forcing their poor white population on, to be slaughtered by hecatombs, to render their own and negro slavery perpetual.

Says the "Metropolitan Record" of July 18th: "The Washington despotism has at length determined on testing its power over the people of the Northern States. The conscription has commenced! For the first time in the history of this Republic, American freemen are to be drafted like the veriest slaves of the most crushing European despotism.

"Will the men of the North submit to this monstrous attempt to fasten upon them a permanent military despotism? Is it possible they are ready to submit to the yoke? We trust not.

"We have no hesitation in saying, that if the people submit to be drafted, to carry out the avowed policy of confiscation and emancipation, that the last vestige of American freedom will be swept away forever. We are heart and soul opposed to the conscription.

"We shall never, under any circumstances, raise an arm against the South. We do not seek to disguise our admiration for that gallant and noble people, and sooner than see them subjected to the abolition yoke, (!)* we would prefer perpetual separation."

In evasion (or defiance) of the law of Congress, punishing resistance to the draft, and of the authorities on whom it devolves to execute that law, such is the present uniform and continuous utterance, not of one organ only, but of the class of Roman Catholic periodicals in this country, of which the ordinary function is to proclaim the dictates of infallibility to several millions of blind, unquestioning subordi-

---

* "Abolition yoke,"—a solecism eminently fit to be uttered by the organ of a power, of which John, the Revelator, said, that of old she trafficked in "wheat, and beasts, and sheep, and horses, and chariots, and slaves, and souls of men."

20*

nates, filling the place and enjoying the privileges, and invested with the governing influence of American freemen.

It may be recollected by many who will read these pages, that a few years ago a thrill almost of terror ran through the Roman Catholic communities of Europe, on waking to a consciousness of the fact that some one or two hundred thousand of the unsuspecting and unsuspected devotees of their religion were annually migrating to this country, of whom a large proportion became gradually alienated, and eventually renounced their allegiance to Rome's spiritual despotism.

No one who is at all acquainted with the character or history of the papacy would be backward to believe that such a leak as this, running out from her numbers and her strength, would be sure to be effectually provided against. Neither would it be matter of surprise to such a one, that no flourish of trumpets was sounded over that effectual provision, as is likely to be the case in a democratic community when anything of public importance is accomplished.

But after the lapse of quiet years, we now have a glimpse of what has been undertaken to check this out-go, and also of its success. In addition to almost all possible appliances to retain among themselves the instruction of their youth, to counteract the influence which our free institutions naturally exert on them, and to retain the membership of their communion in devout and blind and degraded dependence on their appointed priests, an able corps of priestly and editorial authorities have been provided (native Americans, where such could possibly be procured), upon the occurrence of such a juncture in our nation's affairs as that above described, so to put the authority, the sanctity, and the powerful superstition of the papal church in requisition as to insure from the Roman Catholic millions of our Northern population, an unqualified acceptance, as simple truth, of a diabolical tissue of treason and falsehood like that before quoted.

The individual, or conclave, who framed the statements quoted, dictate to those Romish millions, to be received and acted on as true, that the government of the United States as administered by President Lincoln is a " despotism," because it is attempting to keep up its armies by conscription. The ground, and the only ground, for this malignant falsehood, is the despotic nature of the organization and measures, without which military force does not and cannot exist for any purpose whatsoever. It is not

only that said government does not dissolve itself into non-existence at the first challenge of
armed and perjured traitors, but that, after
having exhausted the North by calling for, and
receiving, during the past twenty-eight months
of the war, a million and a half of men, of
whom perhaps one-half are lost to the service
by disease and casualties, and the rest are retiring by the expiration of their terms of enlistment ; and, after having exhausted the North
by an expenditure of money quite in proportion to the number of men, now, at the combined summons of the bloody despots of the
South, their despotized and traitorous partisans
of the North, the lying and pirate-nursing aris-
tocracy of Europe, and the crippled beast upon
the seven hills, the " Washington " government
does not perform voluntary suicide for the tech-
nical objection to its necessary course, that it is
despotic to draft !

Military organization is despotic in form to
the highest degree. It is highly despotic to put
one man under the absolute and almost unconditional authority of another, as is done in every
military company, and without doing which no
military command or power exists. It is despotic to say to citizens outside the army ranks,
you shall so restrict your indulgence in freedom

of speech, and of the press, as not to convey military information to the enemy, nor create insubordination in our army ranks, nor discourage enlistments, nor resist a draft, when ordered.

Yet, all these features of despotism are incident to, and inseparable from, the first and simplest exercise of military strength. Jefferson Davis and his perjured fellows, C. L. Vallandigham, the prince of Ohio Copperheads,* the editors of the "Metropolitan Record" and "Boston Pilot," and the Romish ecclesiastics who dictate what these editors shall, and what they shall not say, all knew and understood this perfectly well when they first combined by military force to attack the United States government. It was an original part of their diabolical contrivance, first, by making an armed assault, to force upon the administration the inevitable and perfectly foreseen necessity of resorting to this formally despotic exercise of power to defend its veriest existence ; and then, as soon as this exercise of power was resorted to, through the agency of these Copperhead and Romish operators in the loyal States, to raise a perfect hallabaloo about the " despotism of the Washington government." This is no fancy operation. It is a war measure of the first importance. If, by this outcry

* See Appendix D.

against the government, a majority of the voters can be deluded into disfavoring voluntary enlistments, and into resisting a draft, then, even at this late day, and after all our victories, and our exhaustion, the national name and life and hope expire by suicide in ignominious chaos; and the leagued powers of Despotism and Popery triumph by malignant guile.

During the self-same hour, in which military power in the Southern Confederacy is forcing every man within its reach, between the ages of sixteen and forty-five, — or sixty, as some of their edicts say,— to take up arms and lay down their lives, if success should require, for the extinction of free government, this accredited mouth-piece of the papacy exhorts his followers to aid and succor the same cause, by not submitting to be drafted into the army which is fighting for the only democratic government on earth; which drafting he amuses himself, and attempts to deceive them, by calling "a monstrous attempt to fasten upon them a permanent military despotism."

In the same style of veracity he goes on not only to call the confiscation of the property and the freeing of the slaves of Rebel despots, "the sweeping away of the last vestige of American freedom," — but he also goes farther to say — what no one could doubt, unless it might be those who were stupid enough to believe what he had already stated—that "he would never, under any circumstances. raise an arm against the South."

He admires the "noble gallantry" of seven and three-fourth millions of abject whites, driven and slaughtered like sheep, by a few thousand slave drivers, for their own purposes; and rather than see the aims of these few cruel, bloody despots defeated, he would "prefer perpetual separation," which is all they ask us at present to grant.

While these more secular organs of the papacy are thus putting light for darkness, and darkness for light, truth for falsehood, and falsehood for truth, despotism for democracy, and democracy for despotism, with the sanction of infallibility before the Catholic millions of our Northern population, at the crisis of the strife, the Pope himself and his highest American prelate are with all earnestness addressing the same class for the same end, but in less simple terms. Their saintly lips do not say, with the "Record," that they desire above all things, a separation of the Union, assured, as they are, that separation and destruction are in this connection perfectly synonymous terms. But they exhort to "peace," which, at this juncture in the progress of the war, and in the ears of those whom they address, they know perfectly well means nothing else but resistance to the United States government, and submission to whatever despot traitors in arms see fit to demand.

X L.

As, in speaking of Europe's complications with the Confederate enemies of free government on this continent, we find it needful to discriminate between the democratic and the despotic classes where despotism is still dominant, so in speaking of the part which papists are taking in this war, we need to distinguish those in whom the love of civil freedom has more controlling force than papal dictation. These are in a position of perplexing trial. They need, and are worthy to receive, a double portion of the sympathy and cordial countenance of freedom's less embarrassed friends.

Whether they can make an extract of the Roman Catholic church, which will bear any traceable resemblance to the original, and will yet be compatible with coexisting and coöperating civil democracy, and which may be called papacy Americanized, remains to be seen. The probabilities are that the Roman Catholic church is too deeply and durably identified with temporal and spiritual despotism to retain a cognizable lineament of its former self, in any adapted form, that will be endurable to a sincere and intelligent adherent of American democracy.

Roger B. Taney, though born and educated a Romanist, was an American in principle; and though for thirty years a coöperator with those whose plots against democracy ripened at last into overt treason, yet it was his friendship for slave-holders, and not his love of the papacy, that made him such.

Major General Wm. S. Rosecrans, though said to have been led by a professedly Protestant chaplain of West Point Academy into the papal communion, has not yet been inoculated with papal politics, or induced to debase the native nobleness of his nature, or abandon the dictates of his superior judgment for the behests of a polluted and suborned ecclesiastical authority. Would that we knew as much were true of his younger brother, the bishop! Each of these represents large classes entitled to our kindest sympathy, and many of them to our gratitude and our confidence, in whose bosoms, with more or less consciousness of what is going on, the war between Democracy and Despotism must rage till either their American politics, or their Romish religion, is given to the winds.*

* See Appendix G.

But what of the French in Mexico? The God of heaven and the revelations of time alone can inform us, save that the wearing anguish of perpetual intestine strife appears likely to mark the future, as it has absorbed the past, of that unhappy country. The papacy, and not slavery has there been and still is the depository of despotic principles and purposes. The leading spirits of that hoary hierarchy have ordained and ordered the forces on the side of despotism, which have kept the portions of this continent, south of the United States, in blood and turmoil ever since their inhabitants attained enough of freedom's fire to throw off the yoke of Inquisitorial Spain. That those papal agencies will be less despotic, or less disturbing, now that France and Austria have united their material military and naval resources in their support, is not to be expected. The forces on the side of freedom in those latitudes have not been nourished and guided, as in the North, by the accepted light and strengthening influence of divine Revelation, and hence are blind and feeble compared with the Northern adherents of freedom's cause. But that they will die out quietly under the impact of the iron heel, after having sustained themselves under every disadvantage for near half a century, is hardly to be expected;

although the blinding, debasing contact of the Romish religion is vastly more efficient to overcome popular resistance, by its paralyzing, festering, infectious corruptions, than any monarchy is to overcome such resistance by military force.

That the brace of first-class despots who have now assumed by favor of the papacy to preside over the destinies of Mexico should attempt to amuse themselves and divert the attention of their restive subjects by bringing on in that neighborhood a first-class conflict upon the standing issue, — Despotism or Democracy, — is perhaps entirely within the limits of probability.

That the ruling intellect in European politics is really aiming to demolish the British power, and, as preliminary to this, with Britain's countenance and Britain's aid, intends to reduce the United States to a condition of feebleness which will render the principal undertaking safe ; that the continental powers are now being conciliated and combined with that intent; that, with the same intent, secret emissaries are inducing England, under an ignored queen and a suborned and dotaged ministry, to launch, equip, and sustain an endless succession of first-class war vessels, under color of a Rebel flag and a mocking pretence of neutrality, to threaten the ports and prey upon the commerce of the United States;

that the hastily-assumed and equivocally-main-
tained neutrality of France and England was,
with the same intent, designed to allow this
country, as far as possible, to exhaust itself in
internal strife, preparatory to foreign assault, —
these are among the facts of current history
that appear to be fast passing from the stage of
occultation.* What the hand of Death or Destiny may do, meanwhile, to mar the perfect-
ness or still the activity of that master brain;
what the liberty-loving mass in its home empire may do to derange the projects of foreign
war; what the exasperated venom of the
Mexican races may yet essay and achieve to
free themselves a second time from a foreign
yoke and groundless usurpation, — these are elements which time alone can supply for a calculation of final results. But that all which

* As well might an artist attempt to fix the form and color of each summer cloud, as a historian to note the *designs* of European rulers. After
Louis Napoleon took armed possession of the city of Mexico, and offered
the crown of a conquered empire to Maximilian, the Archduke of Austria,
with every prospect of its being accepted, but a few weeks elapsed before,
according to one of our best newspaper authorities, the Austrian Emperor
found himself able to combine a European alliance against Napoleon, and
the offered crown was rejected; leaving Mexico, like the elephant drawn in
a lottery, on Napoleon's hands, to be retained, or disposed of as best it
might. Thus brightening, somewhat, the obvious prospect that the American Union would yet survive, not because Europe's despots were less principled against democracy, but because the scheme their late leading intellect had concocted for giving effect to their common principles adverse to
democracy had been frustrated by the virulence of their old home jeal-
ousies

21*

the foregoing pages contain, respecting a despotism upon our borders, will apply to the
offshoot of the French empire on a throne in
Mexico is undeniable; although the boundary
between ourselves and Mexico is not so utterly impalpable as the boundary must needs
be between different segments of the severed
Union; and the question of returning fugitive slaves would not be likely to be an open
ulcer all along that boundary in the case of a
despotism in Mexico, as it would be in the case
of a slave-holding despotism on the soil of the
former Union.

XLI.

GENERAL RÉSUMÉ.

WE have now completed the detailed presentation of the chief topics intended for the present work. We here glance over them collectively.

The passing away of monarchy involves the greatest change to which human society is liable. The rise and establishing of popular government is a delicate and exceedingly critical occurrence, peculiar to the present age of the world. It is necessarily opposed by all that remains of the dying energies of hoary, and hitherto unantagonized, coercive government.

Each of these species of civil society, in its nature, tends to become universal, — as a healthy specimen of animal organization tends to the attainment of its normal dimensions, — and consuming conflict must occur on every border where they come in contact.

This continent was reserved practically vacant for the theatre whereon the new form of social life — "a Church without a Bishop, and a State without a King" — should take its rise.

· This new form of social life is spontaneous in

247

its origin, continuance, and action. It is little else than a negative, — the mere absence of monarchy in a civilized community, with barely latent, organic life enough to render that absence perpetual. Its greatness, its importance, its practical effects, and the points " wherein its great strength lieth," are, to the present time, but very imperfectly understood. The unparalleled growth and affluence of this nation are its novel and peculiar product. The Constitution of these United States is the first great, permanent expression of its new existence.

Defended by surrounding oceans, — which steam and electricity, harnessed by the inventive genius which its own generous nourishings developed, had not yet reduced to insignificance, — it rose to maturity and strength before the family of ancient monarchies became aware of its dangerous antagonism; and, by the time they began to take alarm, their subject millions had become so permeated with the leaven of its presence as to paralyze the arm with which those monarchies would otherwise have struck for its destruction.

But it is not the order of divine procedure that anything designed for universal spread and perpetual prevalence should rise and reign wholly unresisted. Like the hardy oak, this new form of civil life needed a trying blast to give it consistency and strength, to cause its roots to strike down graspingly beneath the surface soil, and to purge its texture from the elements of premature decay.

At an early day in the history of the planting of civilized colonists on this continent, a few ebon seeds of African social life — than which earth has produced none more vicious — were transported, and planted in the rich soil of the watered garden of American freedom. Here they nestled quietly till the first crisis of our nation's birth and infant feebleness were passed; all the time multiplying luxuriantly and combining themselves with elements of power which the old world could not have produced. The sunshine and the showers of this most peaceful and prolific clime gave them colossal proportions and giant strength. Africa supplied the servile mass, and, by its presence, American freemen, who would otherwise have scorned to exercise an authority to which they would not themselves submit, were turned into masters, tyrants, despots. The strongest, most vital, most excellent material which unfettered, bounteous America could produce became quickened with the envenomed life of the darkest, vilest despotism that ever cursed the most barren and remote extremity of the Eastern continent.

Democracy, which affords such unexampled privileges to the individual, presents the lowest, least organic form of civil life. It has neither eyes nor ears nor any other sense by which to take alarm, until it has long felt the pangs of protracted injury.

The viperous despotism, called into existence by the presence of that abject mass from Africa, had already taken into its ravenous maw, digested, and incorporated into itself the whole poor white population of the slave-holding States — had broken their bones, charmed or magnetized, and slabbered over, ready to devour, a vast political party in the North, — part of whom, like the poor whites in the South, prove to have been already digested and appropriated, — and its gory fangs were already darted at the carotid artery of our nation's life, before serious alarm was taken, or any effort made in national self-defence.

XLII.

In approaching some conclusions from the preceding, — conclusions bearing on our future civil duty as loyal citizens, — the connecting of events with causes will not be avoided. -

Where there are slaves, there must be masters. Where there are masters, there must, presently, be despots. Wherever there is a despot, there must be a great and growing submission to his dictation, *or else there will be war,* one or the other, every time the experiment is tried, " now, from henceforth, and forevermore."

When, by the rapid influx of Northern population into California, the Southern despots found themselves baffled in their attempts to add that State to their peculiar dominions, they saw that the time was drawing near at which they must quietly relinquish their usurped control of the general government, or break up the Union. Quietly to relinquish usurped power, is one thing that despots never do. Popular free-

251

dom in the North was so absorbing the influx of
foreign immigration, and was proving itself so
prolific of all that constitutes the resources of a
nation's strength, that it became apparent no
time was to be lost. They were fast sinking
into a powerless minority. Judging others by
themselves, they knew of no reason why the
gross abuses of power which they and their political coadjutors had been practising toward
their opponents should not soon be practised
back on themselves in turn.

They repealed the Missouri Compromise, and
inaugurated the politico-military strife in Kansas,
with some hope of adding that State to their
relatively waning minority ; and with the intention of turning the strife into a general civil
war, in case of failure. They failed in both the
main and substitute design. The "Yankees"
were too shrewd to fight while the general government was yet in the hands of their antagonists. Nothing was left them but to strike for
separation, by all means, and at all hazards.
Their corrupted partisans at the North, acting
under the blasphemed name of Democracy,*
enabled them to retain usurped control of
the general government until its army and
navy had been rendered useless, its treasury

* See Appendix B.

robbed and bankrupted, its arsenals rifled, and all but two of its fortifications in the Southern States clearly within their reach. The hour had come for decisive action. On the peaceable surrender of these two forts hung the momentous sequence of peace or war. Thus near had the Southern despots come to the accomplishment of the first great act in their programme, — separation, without resorting to the arbitrament of the sword. All this had been accomplished during the administration of that prince of Locofocos, James Buchanan, who lay in the hands of his Southern advisers as a pine-knot lies in the maw of an alligator, till everything but the least digestible part of its woody fibre, has been extracted. James Buchanan, who had done every other thing that the Southern despots had desired of him, did not actually issue orders for Forts Sumter and Pickens to surrender, and the traitors, somewhat unexpectedly, found these two places in the hands of men who did not see fit to surrender them unordered, without having a fight first. As Buchanan's administration drew near its close, the traitors, — with whom it had been the main business of his term to coöperate, — having completed all that they could expect to accomplish covertly, having thrown off disguise, confessed their perjury, (and, in "seced-

22

ing," the several Southern States allowed their
real character and design to become apparent,) judged it prudent, one by one, to resign
their offices, leave the capital, and go South;
thus leaving the old knot — from which they
lacked the chemistry to make any farther extract, and which still represented the vital head
of the government — to fall into other hands.
And thus the nation was stayed up from falling
to pieces through Buchanan's unfathomable inefficiency, or treason, as the case may be.

Had Buchanan, like his immediate predecessor, been subject to the influence of strong drink,
probably the traitors could have accomplished
all that they could have desired, in his name,
and by his presidential authority; and the commanders of Forts Sumter and Pickens would
have received orders to evacuate. But when
Buchanan was placed in nomination as the presidential candidate of the Loco-foco party, Frémont,
the opposing candidate, was so popular, and the
accumulated iniquities of the party, under the
then existing administration, had become so
enormous, as to make the result of the election
extremely doubtful; and, in order to secure the
vote of the great State of Pennsylvania, it became necessary for the party to accept her favorite son as their candidate, although in this

respect — his not being liable to be influenced by strong drink — he was not exactly the man that was suited to the purpose for which the real leaders of the party designed to make use of him. They did not dare to restrain him of his liberty, and carry him South with them, because this course would have alienated his and their political coadjutors of the Buchanan stripe in the North.

One trait of the despot, peculiar to the American branch of that family, is, that when he has in hand an enterprise which he likes not to attempt himself, by personal violence, he has a way of raising a mob of the worthless and the desperate, to carry out his plans for him. It appears to be a part of their regular policy, by the absence of schools, and the discouragement of regular industrial avocations for whites, to keep on hand a class of this kind of characters, for such particular occasions. This mode of action gives additional plausibility to their pretence of being Democrats. Some of the most important transactions in the process of seceding the Southern States were carried through by this mode of operating.

But twice in the interim between the presidential terms of Jackson and Buchanan, has their party failed to elect its presidential candidate. And neither of these two only successful candidates who opposed that party survived his inauguration more than a few weeks or months, before he fell in death, — a victim, as the people, in their democratic simplicity supposed, of ordinary disease.

Sure, one there was, who suspected foul play in the first of these instances, and who never doubted it in the second. And now, viewing the cases of sudden demise, so opportune for the party which was aided by them, in the light of their immense importance to the plans which have since been developed, and in the light of the means which have since been resorted to by their authors, to carry these plans into execution, no candid mind, competent to comprehend the evidence in the case, can doubt but that the deaths of those presidents in office were procured by a quiet mode of assassination. Presidents Harrison and Taylor were the only two who ever died in office, and were the only two who succeeded in interrupting the reign of that party dynasty, whose otherwise unbroken prevalence for thirty years has matured in the scenes of treason, desolation, and blood, that now crush our afflicted land.

But aside from the connection in which the

attempt stands catalogued, it is matter of notorious history that a band was leagued, and a
mob prepared, to waylay and dispose of the
present chief magistrate of the nation as he
approached the capitol for inauguration ; at the
same time beleaguering that city and cutting
off communication from the North, taking possession of the city of Baltimore, and forcing the
State of Maryland out of the Union.

Despots of the American type are accustomed
to succeed in whatever they think it worth their
effort seriously to attempt. When they fail, it
is generally safe to conclude that no subtlety,
however acute, no watchfulness, however unre-
mitting, no code of morals, however lax, no application, however assiduous, no exertion, however desperate, and no scheme, however diabolical, could have secured success. The fierceness
of the throes of dying despotism consume the
fountains of whatever is just or gentle in the
individual supporters of that doomed cause.

22*

XLIII.

SEPARATION OF THE DESPOTIC FROM THE DEMOCRATIC ELE-
MENTS IN THE LONG—DOMINANT PARTY — CONDITIONS OF
PEACE.

By moving with celerity on an unusual line
of travel, the President elect arrived in Washington unassassinated, unseized. President Buchanan, in the new hands into which he had
fallen when the traitors let him drop, even favored the peaceful inauguration of his lawfully-
elected successor; and Mr. Lincoln was duly and
peaceably inaugurated at the usual time, though
in the presence of an efficient military guard.

Thus the shattered and almost extinguished
remnant of the United States government passed
from the usurping grasp of the political party
which, headed and handled by a few slave-holding despots, had used that government for their
own selfish and sinister purposes, with little interruption, for the last thirty years; and, during
the last eight of these years, with the scarcely
disguised intention of compassing its destruction.

This relinquishment of power was not at this

time necessary, but voluntary, at least on the part of leaders of that long-dominant party. They supposed they had effectually destroyed the power, and were relinquishing only the shadow of its form. They little doubted that their party adherents in the North were so thoroughly corrupted,* and that the Middle States would find themselves so distracted, that they who laid and launched the plot, with the extreme South already under their undisputed despotism, could dispose of the rest at pleasure; at least, could cast them off at will, and by the aid of their friends, the despotic classes in Europe, could establish a concentrated government that would defy reaction.

On the 23d of April, 1860, the Convention of the long-dominant party met at Charleston, South Carolina, to select a candidate to be voted for by the party, as Mr. Buchanan's successor. The leaders of that party, there assembled, controlled the majority—almost the entire vote—of every Southern State except a trifling defection on the border, and they controlled enough of the Northern States to make the election of their candidate reasonably certain, had they chosen to harmonize and act together as formerly. A few formal compliments, paid by the

* See Appendix C.

Southern despots to prominent Northern partisans, would have secured this harmony, and another Frank Pierce or James Buchanan could have been made president. But such was not the result desired. One Frank Pierce, succeeded by one James Buchanan, had accomplished all that the Southern despots had for such men to do, namely, to put the country in a state of complete preparedness for dissolution. The despotic principles and tastes of the Southrons had become matured. They could no longer endure a fettering combination with even corrupt, venal, traitorous, or deceived Democracy.* If their Northern friends would join them and arm for a consuming conflict with the mother of republics, well and good. If they would go home, and in the several wards and counties manfully resist all efforts to arrest the movements about to be entered on in the South, this service would also be very acceptable. But the unnatural and mutually-loathed union of despotism and democracy that had prevailed ever since

* Robert Toombs publishes a letter in a Georgia paper, saying, — "I can conceive of no extremity to which my country could be reduced in which I would for a single moment entertain any proposition for any union with the North on any terms whatever. When all else is lost, I prefer to unite with the thousands of our own countrymen who have found honorable deaths, if not graves, on the battle-field." As Mr. Toombs is a favorite among the peace men of the North, it might be well that they make a note of his sentiments. — *Boston Journal, September 14th,* 1863.

the rise of the cotton-trade infused vitality and strength into the slave system was now drawing near its termination. The set time for launching a plot for its dissolution had arrived. The old Jackson-Buchanan, or "loaves-and-fishes" party as it was termed by an early critic of its course, had answered well its end; but, like the typical dispensation in religion, at the coming of the great Antitype, was to pass away, or linger out an anomalous and effete existence, opposed alike to the clear light and decisive action of the two great political verities, which, like Paganism and Christianity, were thenceforth to divide the field between them, till the one or the other became extinct.

The separation of the two great elements must of necessity take place in the long-dominant party, as well as in the government proper. As the sundering of the party did not involve the crime of perjury or treason, and would not necessitate war, it was resolved to initiate the grand separation in that party, and the Convention at Charleston was selected as the occasion for doing it. The plan was, by preventing unity of action, to necessitate a plurality of candidates, a division of the party vote, and the consequent success of the opposing candidate, who, as the South were a unit in the hands of their leaders, must of necessity be a sectional candidate, elected by a combination of sectional parties, — this sectional feature must perfect and insure the Southern political unanimity, — then make war on the successful candidate, whoever he might be, before · or after his inauguration, as chance might offer.

The separation in the party, then and there, took place according to the design and purpose of the despot Southrons. They refused longer to consult the interests or to conserve the welfare of the party. In vain the Northern members of the party offered a continuance of their venal services. They were rejected. The separation was so natural, fit, and timely, — especially since the Secession of the States it has appeared so, — that any effort to restore the party-union has been as unnatural and monstrous as would be the attempt to reverse the operation of nature in animal propagation, and endeavor to restore the breathing offspring to its former union with the parent from which it had been separated. The union of slave-mastership and the policy of the Jackson-Buchanan party produced Secession by a process that admits not of being reversed.

If such be the case with the political party that so long held the government in its custody that the two almost became one, what ground, it will be asked, is there to hope that the union of the States can ever be restored? There is no ground for such a hope, not the slightest, so long as Despotism rules the South or any other portion of the States. The first and only, the indispensable and all-sufficient, condition of a restitution of the Union of the States in perpetual harmony, is a revolution of the South from despotism to democracy. All the fighting which the present War has produced or may yet produce, that brings near this result, advances us by legitimate progress toward the attainment of permanent peace. All that fails of bringing near this result, is gratuitous self-inflicted chastisement. It may make us more wise and modest, but in no other way than this can it have any special tendency to terminate the strife.

XLIV.

AMONG the popular masses at the South, the
absence of sagacity to perceive, and of courage
and promptitude to resist, the usurpations of a
military despotism at the commencement of
their secession movement proves those masses
to be devoid of democratic principle, and radically conformed to the condition of the subject
masses of a despotism.* Are their despotic leaders so secure in the rear that they can be reached only by the military destruction of these
masses? Are these masses so devoted to their
leaders that they will not consent to survive
them? If either of these conditions obtain (and
they really are but one), then must the war go
on with unabated destructiveness till the South
is wellnigh consumed, and the North shall have
paid in full the meet penalty for having allowed
a despotic corrupting of the half of its own
home population, and for according the unction

---

* For a vivid and veracious description of the process of seceding, see
The Conspiracy Unveiled. Hunnicutt. Philadelphia. J. B. Lippincott
& Co., 1863.

of its tolerance and the shield of national protection to the deadly asp of Despotism, till its own life's blood had well-nigh paid the forfeit incurred by its indolent credulity.

In view of the enormous cost and suffering which this war is inflicting, North and South, it may be asked whether prompt decisive action, at its origin, could not have arrested and hung its authors, and have left the Southern as well as the Northern masses undecimated and the homes of the former undevastated. Decisive governmental action could probably have arrested the leaders of revolt, and thereby have prevented the progress of the present war; but this would have been only a perilous postponement, — a damming up of a river that would only have increased its strength and fury, as long as the cause continued to act which made despots of the leaders of this revolt. Though the Southern people had been spared their present sufferings, the same causes, continuing to act, would soon produce and place at their head a set of leaders more despotic and desperate than those who are now consigning them to wholesale immolation.

If a bloody or a bloodless revolution could have been instituted in the South, that would have brought the seven and three-fourths millions of non-slave-holding white population in successful conflict with the despot few, who now govern that section with a rod of iron, the present war would have been averted. But such was the amount of power which slavery put into the hands of the despot few, — such was the disadvantage at which slavery placed the seven and three-fourths millions of non-slave-holding whites, — above all, such was the vassal sympathy with the ruling few, into which these non-slave-holding millions were brought by their chronic fear and hate of slaves set free, that nothing but a war which prostrates alike the despot leader and his millions of abject whites can ever clear the soil for the planting of a genuine democracy. Nothing less than the suffering and humiliation which this war is inflicting on the North could have brought its corrupted majority to consent to the establishing of that degree of political equality at the South which is indispensable to the continued existence of democratic, or, in common terms, republican institutions on this continent.

The question here intrudes itself, Must negroes vote? It is impossible to precalculate at what time the elective franchise will become of any practical value to them; or at what time it will be best for us that they should exercise it.

Where there is no compression, there can be no explosion. Where there is an arbitrary deprivation of the practically valuable rights, which, by the equal rule of democratic government, pertain to any class, then and there comes into existence a reacting, explosive force. This force, perpetually conflicting with the original, arbitrary, depriving dictation, the two mutually irritate and strengthen each other till an explosive revolutionary outbreak is the result.

The premature conferring of elective franchise on an abject race, as the negroes now are, and must long be, would only reproduce and multiply ten thousand fold the corrupting and disastrous results of conferring that franchise on the green, ignorant, and politically unprincipled serfs that throng to us from the shores of monarchical Europe.

The prospect of thereby weakening the military strength of the Rebellion, together with the pressing menace of European powers, which could thereby be parried, appear to have induced Mr. Lincoln to proclaim emancipation to the greater part of the Southern slaves.* The demonstrated impracticability of his schemes of deporting the freed negroes, the difficulty of supplying his lack of troops, and the unhealthiness

* See Appendix A.

of many of the locations where troops were necessary to be used, seem to have induced the tardy determination to arm the negroes.

But, whatever may have been the motive which induced the course of action, the first efficient step taken toward preserving the government from the assault made on it from the South was the abolishing of masters,* brought about by emancipating the slaves; and the first step taken toward preventing a recurrence of

* Though there may be men and women in the ranks of those partisans of treason who are voting against President Lincoln's administration, who are ignorant, and hence partially innocent, of the real aim of their party-leaders, yet, beyond dispute, that aim is, singly and solely, by all possible means, to prevent the Emancipation Proclamation from taking effect. Thereby redeeming the institution of slavery from the boiling, burning gulf into which its Southern possessors had thrown it, restoring the Loco-foco organization, with all the Southern slave-holders gratefully owing their preservation to their Northern friends. To accomplish this result, all the infernal zeal that can be expended, all the falsification of facts and principles that may be necessary, and the blood and treasure requisite for two or three years' prolongation of the war, appear to be a moderate price, in the estimation of these precious graduates of the political school in which they have been educated. "*To the victors belong the spoils.*"

Reuben Stout, 60th Indiana Infantry, was shot on Johnson's Island for desertion. He was allowed to go home on furlough. In a confession, made just before his death, he says: —

"After I had been there about two weeks, I was advised by several persons not to go back to the army; they said this was only an 'Abolition war.' I was induced to go to a meeting of the so-called Knights of the Golden Circle, and was made a member of that organization. The obligations of the order bound us to do all we could against the war, — to resist the draft, if one should be made, and likewise to resist and oppose all confiscation or emancipation measures, in every possible way. We were pledged to do all we could to prevent another man or dollar going from the State for the further prosecution of the war."

When a squad attempted to arrest him he killed one of the party the same assault was conferring manhood and elevation of character on the blacks, by admitting them into the army ranks, to fight for their own independence. Failing of either of these two necessary steps, the present war might have continued to the end of time without producing any decisive result in favor of the Union cause. And now, if through their Northern confederates, the Secessionists can succeed in reversing either of these measures of President Lincoln's administration, they have a fair prospect of being the ultimate winners, however the tide of victory may turn in the field.

If the negroes prove to be so effectually freed, and so far elevated above their former condition, that no class of men can again make political use of them as their former masters have hitherto done, doubtless the masses of the Southern whites, freed from their former trammels, and from the powerful presence of the slave-holding class, will adequately educate themselves and put on democracy spontaneously. Especially may this result be expected, when free intercommunication with the North shall have been established.

XLV.

Let us now attempt to gather into focal proximity the leading phenomena of Secession.

Apart from their blind and mad affection for the condensed despotism which slavery presents, and their cringing, suicidal, though unconscious, servility to the leading conservators of this despotism, the non-slave-holding millions of white population in the South had no motive, and could have had no inclination, to engage in the present onslaught against the United States government.

The victory now being contended for by the Southern leaders is a victory over democratic equality, democratic principles, and democratic institutions, and is as much against the rights, prosperity, and prospects of the masses of the people at the South as at the North. And nothing but the arts and coercive power peculiar to successful despots ever placed those South-

ern masses in the ranks of the slave-holders'
army, or still retains them there.

Some light is thrown on the real nature and
aim of Secession — an aim and a nature which
must fashion its future, if it succeeds in prolong-
ing its existence — by the fact that its authors,
and those in behalf of whom these authors act,
prior both to the inception and execution of
their nefarious plan, were in the secure possession of every right, privilege, and power which
democracy could either confer or permit, and
more. They possessed every right, privilege, and
power they or any other set of sane men in their
places could desire or ask, except the privilege
and power of making war and concluding peace
on their own sole, unadvised, unembarrassed
motion, and of adding to the millions of their
slaves at pleasure, by importation or conquest.
This evinces to a demonstration that the true
and real aim of the authors, the leaders, and the
champions of the Secession movement is no
other than to divide their despotism from its former incongruous, embarrassing copartnership
with democracy, — to place it on a basis of its
own, free to pursue its own peculiar aims and
tendencies, by its own peculiar modes of action.

In doing this, they are sure that the iron organization, and the solitary, changeless head of

despotism, will give them incalculable advantage over the loose and changeable executive of a democracy, in the interminable wars that must necessarily follow the achievement of separation. They are also sure that a despotism can always surround itself with its native element,— a state of war,— and that this is so adverse to its antagonist, that, as a democracy, though physically unconquered, it must eventually perish wherever this element permanently prevails.

Slavery is known and admitted to be the corner-stone of the new government to be reared on the Southern fragment of the divided Union.*

The strong and growing determination of the Northern Democrats, after the rupture of the obligations that have hitherto bound them, never again to become the ministers or the menials of a despot in controlling his refractory slaves, is perfectly known, and matter that may be pre-calculated on.

The fact that Southern slaves will be constantly fleeing to the North for protection and freedom is also a matter in respect to which there is no doubt or uncertainty, in case a slave-holding government ever stands by itself on Southern soil.

* See speech of Alexander H. Stephens (Vice-President of the Southern Confederacy, as he is called). George Livermore's Historical Research. A. Williams & Company. Boston: 1863. p. 4.

We have, then, the inevitable conclusion, that the men who are striving to establish this slave-holding kingdom in the South depend for its continuance on perpetual military success, surveillance of the North, and such an extended application of their present policy of "retaliation" * as will compel the ever unwilling democrats of the Northern fragment of our former nation, to guarantee the integrity of their slave system. By how much this state of things will fall short of the military subjugation of the North, it is worth little time or trouble to calculate. And how much is to be done by the Northern partisans of the Southern despots, in bringing about this state of compulsory vassalage, — in substituting the former voluntary coöperative Union,

* It is reported that the Rebels, in view of an immediate bombardment of Charleston, have removed all the Union prisoners taken at Morris Island and Sumter to that city, and also that prisoners have been sent from Richmond that they may be exposed to the danger of the bombardment.—*Journal.*

BALTIMORE, Oct. 30. The *American* has a letter from a responsible correspondent dated Annapolis, Md., 29th, which says the flag of truce boat New York arrived at the Naval School Wharf this morning from City Point, with 180 paroled men; eight of the number died on the boat on its way here.

They actually starved to death. Never, in the whole course of my life, have I seen such a scene as there was presented. They were living skeletons. Every man of them had to be sent to the hospital, and the surgeon's opinion is that more than one-third will die, being beyond the reach of nourishment or medicine. I questioned several of them, and all state that their condition has been brought on by the treatment they have received at the hands of the Rebels. They have been kept without food, and exposed a large part of the time without shelter of any kind.

by a severed state, and a compelled rendering
of such subordinate help as is indispensable to
the preservation of their slave property, — is
also unimportant, and of no modifying influence
on the final result. The bitterness of final military subjugation will be little alleviated by the
reflection that the Southern despots, who imposed it, could not have succeeded without the
aid of corrupted and traitorous partisans in our
midst.*

* There is something damningly dishonest in the professions and the practices of those Northern men, of the Vallandigham, Wood, and Seymour
school, who are unfriendly to the United States government as now administered, and yet refuse to put their necks directly under the yoke that Jeff.
Davis is imposing on the people of his realm. They are, obviously, aiming
to barter their countrymen, and their country, to that modern Nero, for
positions near the throne which he is wading through "blood to the horses'
bridles" to establish.

XLVI.

SOMETHING more than appears at first view can be learned respecting the true nature and aims of Secession, by looking at the deliberate sacrifices by which its authors, from the first, proposed to attain their ends.

When we look at the movement in the light of these sacrifices, their extent, their deliberateness, the unreserved freedom with which they are offered, and the comparative insignificance and doubtful worth of the proposed returns, — it may almost be doubted whether the movement had really any other motive than a disposition, on the part of its authors, to destroy everything that they had the opportunity and the power to reach and ruin.

The first great item in this bill of sacrifices is, our nationality. It was held in common by North and South. It had a history, radiant with the wisdom and prowess of our common patriot sires. It had a prospective future, glowing with a gorgeousness of promise almost beyond belief. Though young in years, and novel in the political basis on which it rose, it had attained a respectability and influence abroad which we would have exchanged with no other nation. It was unconquerable by any external force that could be brought against it. An easy exercise of its military strength was sufficient to defend and vindicate the rights of itself and of its citizen, wherever threatened. The benefits it conferred on its citizens at home were more ample, rich, and costless than had ever before been conferred by any human government. It made our country the desired home and refuge of the oppressed of every land. It was the beacon-light of popular liberty to a tyrant-ridden world. Add to these considerations the unutterable affection with which every virtuous patriot cleaves to the institutions, as well as to the soil, of his native land, and multiply the sum by the tens of millions of its blessed and contented population. All this is utterly and certainly destroyed by the first act of the purposed separation. Large fragments of the ruin may, or may not, remain; may, or may not, retain some traces of the great original; no one knows, and, of all others, no one appears to care less than the Secessionist, how this may be.

To the destruction of our nationality add the individual pecuniary sacrifice at which this War has hitherto been, and is yet to be, carried on. Nine hundred millions of dollars is the computed war debt of the Union government at the end of the first two years of war. Add to this the millions that have been raised by war-tax, the many millions that have been voluntarily contributed for hospital and other necessary war expenses, the loss of income suffered by abstracting an average of nearly a million and a half of Northern men from their customary industrial avocations, add a proportionate outlay for the remaining years of the War, of whatever number they may be, and you have, approximately, the Northern half of the pecuniary sacrifice at which this fratricidal strife is carried on. Instead of estimating the Southern portion of the cost as nearly parallel, you might as well consider that the Southern army is made up, to a great extent, of men who were accustomed to earn very little by their industry, before the war begun, and are accustomed to receive little or nothing of real value for their coerced services in it, while it lasts. But to balance this reduction of the expenses of the war to

24

the Southern party, reflect that their section
has to sustain the havoc and devastation of both
armies present on their soil; that all commercial intercourse with the outer world is absolutely
cut off, except what is carried on by blockade
running,— a process in which three ventures cut
of four are captured, and the successful one has
to demand and receive a price that will pay for
the whole; that industrial avocations and the
productions of the soil are reduced to the limits
of what will barely sustain life; that their
slaves, whom they valued so highly as to stake
everything else on the chance of preserving
them in slavery, have already been, or must
soon be, emancipated to a man, and you will
perceive that there was more truth than poetry
in the statement of " Vice-President" Stephens
to the planters, that, " in case they did not succeed in securing their independence, nothing
which they possessed would be worth anything."
In other words, it will be seen that the War, as
planned by its Southern authors, was designed,
if unsuccessful, to involve the blank annihilation
of the property value of everything possessed
by Rebel owners.

Two considerations modify the first view of
the incalculable pecuniary sacrifice so freely offered up by the authors of Secession. First, they

put a very light estimate on all pecuniary considerations. One efficient means, by which the Southern mind has been excited to war upon the North, has been the ridicule and contempt thrown on the " Yankees " for their overweening love of property. This contempt for pecuniary considerations in the Southern mind, arises first, from the natural recklessness of one who, from never having earned property, has little appreciation of its worth; second, from a barbaric indifference to that elevated civilization of which property is the basis, — this trait having been derived by the whites from their social participation in the uncivilized character of the blacks; third and last, but not least, it is the exhibition of that contempt for all other considerations, which naturally occupies the mind devoted to the pursuit, exercise, and enjoyment of despotic power.

In making, then, a just estimate of the incalculable pecuniary sacrifice at which the authors of this Rebellion proposed to purchase their triumph over our republican institutions, let us make all due allowance for their peculiar disesteem for the pecuniary value of what all other claimants for the rank of civilized people esteem as highly valuable.

Second : A second consideration that modifies

the first view of this incalculable pecuniary sacrifice, is the shade of uncertainty that rested on
the fact of its being finally, and wholly, exacted.
If Mr. Buchanan, as there was doubtless very
strong reason to expect he would do, had ordered the evacuation of Forts Sumter and Pickens, if, as there was perhaps every possible
assurance would be the case, Mr. Buchanan's
party in the North had stood up boldly and
blindly for the destruction of the Union, and
the erection and immunity of a Southern Despotism, then the negro property would not all at
once have been lost, and perhaps much of the
present war expenses of the North and South
would have been for a time postponed.* But
giving due weight to this peradventure, we have
still the absolute certainty that the original design and determination of the despot originators
of the revolt was, if they could not attain their
end at less expense, TO SACRIFICE THE WHOLE.

This last qualifying consideration, and, per-

---

* Had the authors of this Rebellion succeeded in reducing the people of
the whole country to the condition of abject dependence in which the
Southern masses have found themselves, and had they succeeded in doing
this before the torpid democracy of the Northern States became alarmed,
and before blood had been shed, then, according to the logic of all past
time, whatever of disaster and suffering might have been incurred in rendering their usurped supremacy perpetual would have been chargeable, not
to the despots themselves, who should fight "to maintain necessary and
wholesome government," but to the "rebellious turbulence" of their subjects
who should fight to rid themselves of 'wholesome and necessary restraints.'

haps, to some extent, the one preceding it, apply also to the third great item in the bill of sacrifices deliberately offered by the authors of the present war, which is, the sacrifice of human life which it involves.

The data are not at hand from which to estimate the expense in human life at which this terrible War has been thus far prosecuted, much less can we now calculate the bill of mortality which will be presented at its close.

The Union government has called for and received for military and naval service a million and a half of men, perhaps a few more or less, but very nearly that number. During the two years and two months of the War already passed, an average of about 800,000 men must have been in the field. The Rebels, by their sweeping conscriptions, without regard to past precedent or future prospects of keeping their number good, have kept up a force two-thirds as large as the Union force, and for a part of the time exceeding that proportion. Modern implements of war have been destructive to life and limb beyond a parallel. The fighting has been frequent and severe, though often undecisive. The larger number of our men has of course exposed us to a heavier loss than the Rebels. A lack of acclimation in the Southern fields which

24*

they have occupied has acted against the health and lives of our men. The improved and perfected sanitary regulations and appliances of the Union army have been of immense effect in saving our men. The necessary or needless lack of these, on the Rebel side, has brought the actual loss to the two about equal. Perhaps our assaulting of their Mississippi fortifications is turning the balance in their favor. The licensed slaughter of all Union men within the reach of Rebel marauders adds an item to the whole. From a quarter to half a million of the most valuable lives, men in their early prime, have doubtless already been destroyed in the progress of this War. Multiply by this the distress and sorrow of a circle of loving hearts that ached and bled for each. If figures, or words can be found, adequate to express the footing of these three items of this bill of the sacrifices, then can we approximate the cost at which the perjured leaders of this inhuman treason proposed to purchase their exemption from all incumbering contact with the mildest and most humane and liberal form of civil society ever realized.

What light does this computation of their deliberate, intelligently preconcerted sacrifices throw on the nature of their aim. The two of necessity are consonant and accordant. What is the aim that accords with such means of attaining it? What is the proposed diversity from their former civil state that justifies the outlay of this unutterable cost in arriving at it? The picture before us exhibits the infuriate spirit of all relict barbarity, committing wholesale demolition on the producers, and the products, of modern civilization. It is the demon of ancient Despotism, long driven from his throne, returning, " with seven other spirits more wicked than himself," to reduce the outgrowth of all modern principles to that condition of narrowness and poverty that suits a restoration of his reign. The annihilating destruction of property, and of national character, strength, and resources, and the fiend-gloating oblation of life and love and hope, are not so much the dreaded but necessary means of attaining a precious end that compensates the cost, as they are themselves the end, subordinate in ultimate importance, only, to the restoration of a despotism designed and fitted to perpetuate the desolation its advent has induced.

The bill of inexpressible costs, deliberately incurred by those who laid and launched the plot for the destruction of the United States government, proves that the present war is no accident, the dictate of no mere caprice. Men do not consign their own country, their own section, and their own homes, to devastation, and their own friends and neighbors and sons to wholesale immolation, from mere caprice, unless their African associations have reduced' them to the level of Dahomians. The present War is taking place under the action of the deepest principles and the most abiding laws that govern man's individual or associate action. In case of Southern success, and the achieving of Southern independence, the same law that induced the present War and the transpiring sacrifice would prompt a continual repetition of the war and sacrifice, till the last remnant of the hated democratic government shall have been eradicated from the continent. In case of Rebel failure, under the action of the same abiding law of inimical antipathy to all democratic rule, as little almost as possible, besides bones and ashes, is designed to be left, to grace the triumph, or requite the outlay, of the friends of civil freedom.

It is not more the cause of this country and of this generation than it is the cause of all nations and of all time, that is now being fought out on American soil, between the friends and the enemies of civil freedom ; therefore this

ignoring of all human ties, on the part of the
latter, this insatiate greed to ruin all that they
cannot permanently rule.

We are told that some serpents have the ability to fascinate their prey. Few facts in natural life fail to exemplify some active principle in
the moral and social world. So we see this spirit of fiendish destructiveness, this unmitigated
antagonist, not only of democratic equality of
rights, but of all human happiness and prosperity, fascinates into an insane fondness for itself,
first, and most naturally, the female portion of
its master-class; second, and most fatally, the
poor white portion of its own Southern community, whom it has kept in permanent deprivation of everything but naked existence on the
cheapest rations; third, last, and least excus-
ably, those political partisans at the North,
drunk from the orgies of former political triumph and partisan excesses, beyond the possibility of ever conceiving a purer desire, or a
nobler design, than to achieve the overthrow
of those whom they elect to treat as political
enemies, though patriotism and peace, prosperity, national existence, and the star of hope, go
down in bloody chaos and eternal night at their
discomfiture.

It is the necessary infirmity of all democracy, that the most ignorant and incompetent, the constitutionally selfish, incapacitated, malign, and perversely active, as well as the able, devoted, and patriotic, must have an equal chance of acting on the destinies of the civil State. But that the former classes should combine, with no other creed, doctrine, or political principle than that of dividing the incomes and patronage of civil employment among themselves, and to this end the electing at every cost of the candidate of their own nominating,—this is a misfortune, so far as history shows, peculiar to the American Republic.

That, after thirty years of success and consolidation, this ruling combination, under the blind and fatuitous assumption that they are thereby to perpetuate their power, should sell themselves, and their hitherto ruling influence, to a clique of the boldest despots, professing to aim at nothing but the enslavement of subordinates, and exultingly gloating at the repast, as they clutch the vitals and drink the life-blood of the nation, — this results from criminal delinquency on the part of better men than themselves,—a delinquency which they, who are guilty of it, and their unoffending sons and daughters are now atoning for in tears and treasure, and are washing out with blood.

Good and evil originate and abide together in every human community. But that, among the rich privileges which republican government confers upon its possessors is the privilege of perpetually postponing with impunity all political strife between the evil and the good, is a fundamental error, and leads to the accumulation of the arrearages of that unpleasant and neglected duty, into an avalanche like that which is pouring on the virtuous portion of the nation at such an hour as this.

It is not transcending the legitimate boundaries of political, historic inquest to note that no small encouragement has been given to the present onslaught on the government and life of the nation, by those infidel diddlers who have so industriously inoculated the Northern mind with non-resistant and no-punishment sentiments that it was matter of military calculation that a certain portion of the Northern people would "lie supinely" still, while despots "bound them hand and foot," and cut the throats of such as they did not see fit to consign to active servitude.

The permitted self-appropriation of the terms "Democracy," and "Democratic" by the pro-slavery, pro-southern politicians of the North, has exerted an immense influence with the uninformed and the unreflecting at home and abroad, in bringing the country to its present imperilled and distressed condition. And every man professing Union sentiments, who by his practice still sanctions that appropriation of those terms, to that extent becomes accessory to the traitor's crime.

The artful orators and editors of the South have, from the first, used only that form of speech which ignores entirely the possible dissolving of the joints and bands by which their subordinates are incorporated into one living, acting organism, under its despotic head. Northern partisans of the despots, of course, adopt the same rule of utterance, and the Union people, and the government itself, have been too ready to allow this form of expression respecting the Southern people. Those despot leaders speak of "subjugation or success as their only alternative," and say that "annihilation and subjugation mean the same thing." Their views in this regard are doubtless correct, so far as themselves individually and their own dominating class are concerned. And their annihilation is probably the first indispensable step toward a restoration of peace. But that the seven and three-fourths millions of Southern white population, who occupy the place, and participate in the spirit, only of the subject masses of a grinding despotism would consign themselves to annihilation rather than become reformed into a community of equal rights, — a sincere democracy, — is an undemonstrated proposition which no one believes to be true, not even those who never speak as if its falsity were possible. The absence, root and branch, of the whole system of negro slavery, and the annihilation of the despotic master-class from among them, will work wonders in preparing the way for vast, radical, rapid, and enduring changes in the political faith and practice of the masses of white population at the South.

25

XLVII.

WE now glance back, prepared to estimate more perfectly than at any previous point the true value of what will have been found to be a leading doctrine in what this book contains; namely, that the despot and the democrat are two distinct kinds of being in the civil world, as irreconcilably and unconvertibly different as it is possible to make those who possessed originally the same natural physical and mental constitution. In other words, as stated at first, the change from despotism to democracy, or the reverse, is the greatest secular change to which the human constitution is liable, whether the individual or the community be the subject on which the change is considered to have passed. So that the democrat and the despot, the friend and advocate of democracy on the one hand, and the friend and advocate of despotism on the other hand, are as inconvertibly different, as irreconcilably antagonistic to each other, in the civil world, as it is possible for two individuals to become, each of whom started with the same conformation of body and of mind.

We use the qualifying term secular, in speaking of this difference, this change, in order to distinguish it from the change of character which separates between the individual who does, and the individual who does not, voluntarily submit himself to the moral government of God.

We would here, without discussing its merits, suggest the inquiry, whether there is not, in this age and section of the world, a marked disparity between the friends of democracy and the friends of despotism, in respect to the proportion which each class contains of those who believe in, and aim sincerely to obey, the revealed Scriptures.

We would still bear in mind that the despotic class are of two grades,—the governing and the governed; the ambitious and selfish and potent few, and the foiled and defeated and circumvented, but still undemocratic, many.

We would here reflect on what needs no extended discussion, such is its obviousness, — that any considerable aspiration after office, power, or perhaps after permanently accumulated wealth,* is essentially a despotic exercise, radically inimical to democracy, inimical to that consenting equality of privilege which is the soul and essence of democracy — and constitutes the nascent struggle by which the radically despotic member of the abject grade in a despotism breaks the shell of his chrysalis, to come forth a full-fledged, breeding specimen of the ruling class, as inconvertibly fixed in despotic principles as devils are in sin.

Here, evidently, is one of the greatest perils of a maturely democratic State, namely, in the natural ambition of the individual to possess himself of a fragment from the crumbling prerogative of despotic power, especially as the vigilant, restless, persevering, and persistent enterprise which this ambition produces, stands out in uncompensated contrast, and destructive antagonism, against the modest, unambitious self-restraint which characterizes, and constitutes the leading element in, true democracy.

Thus in the ordinary routine of electing civil officers in a democratic State, the most despotically inclined come to the surface naturally, and

---

* That "cursed love of gold," which the Father of our Country foresaw, would be a chief source of peril to the permanency of our government.

those employed in the activity peculiar to the nascent despot are almost the only ones that stand any chance of being elected. Thus the indiscriminated and the indiscriminating attachment to principles of popular freedom and democratic equality, on the one hand, becomes pitted against the restless energy of the individual despot, on the other hand ; and hence arises an element of strife, if not the leading element of strife, in the greater number of our popular elections, unless it be when two candidates who are both more aspiring than democratic get to contending with each other over the coveted preferment. And every succeeding success of candidates thus procuring themselves to be elected leaves their kind and class encouraged and strengthened, and leaves the indiscriminating lovers of popular liberty, over whom they triumph, more cowed and abject. Thus the democratic community, under the modern self-electing agency of office-seekers, yearly approximates more and more nearly to the constitution of a despotic state of society, which is characterized by a division into the ruling few and the abject many.

I find myself sometimes instinctively calling for some coercive force wherewith to extend the

25*

principles of democratic freedom. But such an idea is absurd. It is but a lingering remnant of despotic life enlisting itself in favor of a changed and, to it, an unnatural aim. Democratic principles, the love and practice of popular freedom, are of their own essential nature, necessarily self-propagating, purely spontaneous in their spread. To curb and curtail the usurping power of despots, to afford to popular masses time and space and facilities for self-education and elevation, and to set before them present examples of an imperative demand for, and a self-restrained contentment with, democratic equality of civil position and privilege, appears to be all that can be done for propagating principles of democracy beyond the sphere in which an individual or a people is alone responsible.*

This kind of protection and encouragement may be given to the subordinate classes in the Seceded States, in the absence of slavery, and if a rising spirit of democracy and self-improvement appears and develops itself, as, aided by something of immigration, doubtless will be the case, then this continent is secure and sacred to democracy. Otherwise, and especially if sla-

---

* All the democratic principles or practices propagated by dictation, are only such as are received by the abject class in a despotic state of society over which that dictating power presides.

very is permanently replanted, the seeds and source of civil despotism remain, consuming conflict is inevitable, and the pining anguish of intestine strife, or fratricidal war, is perpetuated and must prevail, till the sickened nationality rots away. For if these seeds and this source of despotism survive their present low and imperilled predicament, there is little hope that they will ever become extinct; and as for the spirit of freedom which is inimical to all despotism, there is no reason to believe that it will die out from this its Heaven-prepared birth-place and home, until it shall have died out elsewhere from off Jehovah's footstool.

As the war progresses, and, more especially since the military power of the "Confederacy" begins to show exhaustion, and Southern Unionists begin to speak out, and tell what they know, as R. S. Donnell, of the "Raleigh State Journal," has recently [August 20th, 1863] done, it becomes undeniable as a matter of history, that the plan to divide the Union was formed by leading Southerners many years ago, and that many measures of government and legislation, like the repeal of the Missouri Compromise, the framing of the Fugitive Slave Law, —

even back to the building of the forts that guard
the Southern ports, — and especially leading
measures adopted by the ruling political party,
and the final rupture of that party at its convention at Charleston, were steps taken with direct reference to the intended separation, and
with the design to make that separation easy
and certain.* As matter of history, independent
of any argument this work elsewhere contains,
I now desire to refer to this admitted fact, and
to make it the basis of the following argument.

To form a plan of operations so momentous
and so vast, to impress the disposition and purpose of its execution on an extensive and ruling
class of men, in many and diverse States, to
transmit the plan and purpose from generation
to generation, as these Southern leaders have
done ; to interlock their damnable treason in
disguise with the most important acts of the
government and of the people of the nation
through a course of tens of years, to say nothing of the herculean strength and almost su-
perhuman activity which these leaders have
developed and displayed since the War began,
— and this, too, with only the passive support of
popular masses whose every real interest was in
point blank hostility to the course their leaders

* See Mason's letter to Davis, — Appendix C.

induced them to pursue, — demonstrates these Southern leaders of the Rebellion to possess executive talents and governing abilities which never have been, or can be, either produced or perpetuated in individual democrats, or in a democratic community.

The confiding quiet of a democratic state of society, while it affords the amplest scope for self-elevation by the arts of peace and useful industry, affords neither cause nor opportunity for developing talents parallel to those which the Southern leaders have displayed.*

The absence of these talents, and the absence of the aims and avocations which constitute their peculiar exercise, — the absence of a fiery ambition that would consume every endeared thing but its naked self, would immolate its countrymen, and leave its native land a blackened waste, in the pursuit of despotic power, — this is the great deficiency in " Yankee " constitution and character, which renders the democratic population of the North so insufferably offensive in modern times to the nostrils of Southern men. But thanks be to God, there are more than seven

---

* The nearest approach that is made to this will probably be in the case of some stray villain who makes it his business to prey upon the possessions and rights of others, and defy the law. In this line of action, extraordinary abilities are sometimes developed; after the manner of the Kansas Quantrell, and the guerrilla, John Morgan.

and a half millions of Southern men who are incapable of appreciating, or even perceiving, this offensiveness, — men to whom a taste of democratic equality of rights and privileges, and an introduction to the arts of peace and industry as they have become developed in the truly democratic North, in the absence of slaves and their despot masters, and of fear of servile insurrection, will be as life from the dead.*

If the present War succeeds in emancipating these millions of Southern whites from the grinding despotism under which they have been crushed from generation to generation, till they had become so conformed to their impoverished and depressed condition as to be hopelessly unconscious of their wrongs, it will have added another brilliant wreath to the diadem of Liberty, — will have given that turn to the tide of victory which must render her dominion on this continent perpetual and supreme.

The exhaustless resources and massive popular strength which gather spontaneously to democracy must be relied on, in the yet unended conflict between the two, to counterpoise

---

* Tyrants hate democrats, their subjects never, except so far as they have been trained like apes to imitate the very sentiments and sensations of their keepers.

the talent for command peculiar to the champions of despotism.

A moiety of the peculiar ability that, in the space of a few weeks, successfully commanded the millions of Southern whites, who supposed themselves to be democratic members of a democratic community, into the subordinate ranks of a consolidated despotism of the most bloody and inhuman kind, had that moiety been possessed on the other side, would have frustrated the current treason in somewhat the style in which its prelude, nullification, was brought to nought.

The issue, in the existing War, is between Despotism and its supporters on the one hand, and Democracy and its adherents on the other hand. These two belligerents have each the seat of its power and the body of its forces, mainly, but not entirely, the former at the South, the latter at the North. Each belligerent has some friends on the territory controlled by its antagonist; and the one that, by the aid of its absent friends, succeeds in raising an important diversion (producing a permanent revolt) on the soil and among the adherents of its antagonist, must be the final winner. The same was true before the strife at arms commenced, is true while that strife lasts, and will continue to be true when that strife is over.

Each belligerent has its forces mainly on the section of this country which it controls, but Europe, Africa, and Asia, heaven, earth, and hell, are all interested and taking active part in the conflict. Every month the contest approaches, and the combatants divide, more and more obviously near upon the line that separates between righteousness and iniquity.

The successful artifice by which John Morgan, after such a course as he had run, succeeded in surrendering himself, unhurt, a prisoner of war in the interior of Ohio, the inhuman plan, and still more inhuman execution of that plan, by which Davis rids his dominions of those who are unfriendly to him, putting them in the van of the hottest fights, and hanging as traitors all who object to being thus disposed of, the style in which Generals Baker, Lander, McCook, and others of whom Davis was afraid, have been put out of the way, the African style in which Lawrence, Kansas, was treated,* — these in contrast with the guilelessness that is ever permitting the success of such artifices as that of Morgan and the rest, together with the self-restraint that leaves Davis's dominions so long and so extensively uninterfered with, give the

---

* The Richmond *Examiner* justifies the Lawrence massacre as a "gallant and perfectly fair blow at the enemy." — *Boston paper.*

characteristic lineaments of the two belligerents.*

The idea of destroying Davis's government in the estimation and confidence of the Southern people appears never to have entered into President Lincoln's plan of operation. Perhaps it would have availed nothing if it had. Even if it had entered into that plan, and had been availing, the despotic organism over which Davis presides, like polyps of certain species, when beheaded, would spontaneously supply its deficiency, and live on. But the idea of destroying the present administration in the esteem and confidence of the Northern people, and the (to them at least) apparent feasibility of the project, have doubtless presented a prominent object of aspiration and effort, and a prominent source of hope and encouragement to the Rebel leaders.

According to the light we now possess, had the present administration shown itself to any considerable extent more feeble and hesitating than it did, the loyal masses of its supporters would have become so doubting and disheartened, and the Northern friends of treason would have become so bold and active, that Secession would have had an early triumph; or the War

* See Appendix D.

26

would have been protracted to a point at which reunion would not have appeared worth contending for.

On the other hand, had the present administration, at an early period of the struggle, rung out a clear analysis of the situation, and a decided policy, after the manner of Gen. Rosecrans' letter to the Ohio legislature; had it adopted and pursued a military course, obviously, inexorably, with ever-deepening stress, and by the use of all availing means, bent on the achieving of its proper aims, instead of countermanding the orders of Fremont, Hunter, and Burnside, and catering to the semi-secessionists of the Border States till the exhaustion and havoc of eighteen months of war, apparently spent in demonstrating the mildness of the government, had quenched the fervor of united patriotism which was kindled by the first attack on Fort Sumter, — thus leaving the stagnant and discouraged feelings and opinions of the people to be tampered with by such demagogues as C. L. Vallandigham, D. W. Voorhees, Fernando Wood and the Toucey Seymours, — might not this administration have so led the Northern people, instead of waiting to be led by them, as to have diminished the blood-and-treasure expenses of the War by one or two years' expenditures? This is a question for later days to answer. And the right and final answer, it may be, will not be given before another century has shed its light on the points in which a virtuous monarch and an equally virtuous chief magistrate of a democratic people agree to differ.

Something of the same light, perhaps, also, should be allowed to fall on the inquiry, whether the statesmen of the old Whig school, in their unrelaxed and undying antagonism to the progressive corruption and traitorous depravity of their opponents, instead of allowing themselves to be finally discomfited and laying themselves down in quiet graves, either beneath or above the sod, should not, one and all, have left their homes at Bladensburg, if need required it, sooner than have left the envenomed progeny of Calhoun and his political party thus to immerse the nation in its self-shed blood, and thus to precipitate a peril to the cause of Liberty more to be dreaded than the sacrifice by which the threatening disaster is being turned away.

But the delinquency of these statesmen, and the resulting sacrifice and peril, are putting a purer and more grateful song in the lips of those who, with something of the faith of ancient Miriam, are disposed to praise their people's Great Deliverer.

When this dreadful War shall have ended, — when this conspiracy of home-born traitors shall have been effectually put down, and this confederation of foreign despots, potentates, and powers, shall have been defeated, — then will there go up one general shout of joy, — joy more heartfelt, more wide-extended and enduring, than human hearts ever before experienced, or human tongues ever uttered before. "Ethiopia shall stretch out her hands unto God," and the emancipated millions of our Southern white population will soon send back the sound.

APPENDIX.

A. (Page 267.)

THE following extract from a letter addressed, March 25th, 1862, to a Senator who had moved in the Senate of the United States the compensated emancipation of slaves in the District of Columbia, presents one feature of the process of emancipation : —

SIR : — A proposition to emancipate the slaves of the unseceded States, with a compensation to masters, being prominently before Congress, having had extended acquaintance among Southern men, and some experience in the management of slaves, and having been for the six years last past a voter in your State, I ask leave to lay before you briefly a few reflections on this subject.

I believe it to be admitted as true, among those whose experience best entitles them to know, that slave-labor is unprofitable, except where employed in the producing of some one great staple commodity readily marketable for cash.

Since the introduction of tobacco-culture into the new States of the West, slave-holding in the northernmost of the Slave States has been decidedly unprofitable ; and must have been abandoned, had it not been for the profit derived by selling off the increase of the slave population to the Cotton States.

Now, the present War either will, or will not, destroy the slave-market in the far South. If that market is destroyed, slave property in the other States thereupon becomes, with few and seeming exceptions, utterly and notoriously worthless ; and any proposal to pay masters out of the United States treasury for relinquishing their claim on it, is little else than fraudulent. If, on the other hand, slavery in the Cotton States is not destroyed, then slaves in the Border States have still a pecuniary value; and by proposing to compensate masters for releasing them, government simply enters the market as a competitor, to keep up the price. . . . .

All that is vital to our national existence and prosperity, is involved in the prompt and utter extinction of slavery in the cotton latitudes.

B. (Page 252.)

The following article on political nomenclature, was published in the "Portland Press," of July, 1863 : —

A more damning falsehood never was palmed off on a pack of fools, than that the pro-southern, pro-slavery politicians of the North are not the radical and necessary enemies of all democracy.

No two things in nature are more irreconcilable, invariably and eternally antagonistic, than despotism and democracy. One or the other must perish, wherever they come in contact.

Slavery is the darkest, densest form of despotism.

The Southern Confederacy, founded on slavery, begotten of slavery, living for, aiming at, tending toward, and ending in, nothing else but slavery, already presents the world, in this third year of its nascent existence, with the fiercest and most unmitigated form of despotism that there is this side of Dahomey. Its European abettors, with Louis Napoleon at the head and the "London Times," at the tail, are the dregs of Europe's *effete* despotic class. But these Northern sympathizers with, and aiders of, the precious combination, forsooth we are told are "Democrats" !

Now the mere sound of the words democrat and democratic sways the opinion of large masses of European minds, controls the political faith and action of the principal portion of our immigrants and of immense multitudes of our home-born voters ; and as long as Union men, democratic supporters of a democratic government, allow and aid the bald and brazen advocates of everything that pertains to despotism to adorn themselves and delude their dupes with the purloined and self-appropriated title, " Democrats," so long will conclusive reasoning on political subjects before the public mind be impracticable ; out of the resulting fog and confusion, designing demagogues will have an easy task to make the worst appear the better argument ; if our armies are victorious in the field, wavering multitudes will join the side of victory, without any apprehension of the nature or importance of the principles that win ; and while the war continues, hundreds of thousands of honest and right-minded men like Butler and Corcoran will have to fight and toil and suffer for years, before they will begin to see that Jeff. Davis and his comrades are not entirely innocent, while they call themselves " Democrats " and Abraham Lincoln a "despot," — and all this because our political writers and speakers and thinkers lack the grace and courage to call things by their right names.

Abraham Lincoln is a democrat. His administration is a democratic administration. The only opposite of democratic is despotic. Jefferson Davis is a despot. His administration is a despotism. The men who support and favor it are in favor of despotism. When they shall have done with the United States, if they do not get used up before that time, the United States will be a despotism, and all — as many as dwell within its boundaries — who are not in favor of despotic government will be compelled to keep their mouths shut, or do worse.   T. S. G.

C. (Page 259.)

The following is a letter from Frank Pierce to Jeff. Davis, which was originally published in Concord about a week ago.

As its authenticity has not been disputed, we may safely conclude that it is genuine.

CLARENDON HOTEL, January 6, 1860.

MY DEAR FRIEND : — I wrote you an unsatisfactory note a day or two since. I have just had a pleasant interview with Mr. Shepley, whose courage and fidelity are equal to his learning and talents. He says he would rather fight the battle with you as the standard bearer in 1860 than under the auspices of any other leader. The feeling and judgment of Mr. S. in this relation is, I am confident, rapidly gaining ground in New England. Our people are looking for the " Coming Man," one who is raised by all the elements of his character above the atmosphere ordinarily breathed by politicians, — a man really fitted for this emergency by his ability, courage, broad statesmanship and patriotism.

Colonel Seymour (Thomas H.) arrived here this morning and expressed his views in this relation in almost the identical language used by Mr. Shepley. It is true that in the present state of things at Washington and throughout the country, no man can predict what changes two or three months may bring forth. Let me suggest that in the morning debates of Congress, full justice seems to me not to have been done to the Democracy of the North. I do not believe that our friends at the South have any just idea of the state of feeling hurrying at this moment to the pitch of intense exasperation between those *who respect their political obligations*, and those who have apparently no impelling power but that which fanatical passion on the subject of domestic slavery imparts.

Without discussing the question of right, — of abstract power to secede — I have never believed that actual disruption of the Union can occur without blood ; and if, through the madness of Northern Abolitionists, that dire calamity must come, *the fight-*

ing will not be along Mason and Dixon's line merely. IT
WILL BE WITHIN OUR OWN BORDERS, IN OUR OWN STREETS,
BETWEEN THE TWO CLASSES OF CITIZENS TO WHOM I HAVE RE-
FERRED. *Those who defy law and scout constitutional obligations will, if we ever reach the arbitrament of arms,* FIND OC-
CUPATION ENOUGH AT HOME. Nothing but the state of Mrs.
Pierce's health would induce me to leave the country now, although it is quite likely that my presence at home would be of
little service. I have tried to impress upon our people, especially in New Hampshire and Connecticut, where the only elections are to take place the coming spring, that while our Union
meetings are all in the right direction and well enough for the
present, they will not be worth the paper upon which their reso-
lutions are written, unless we can overthrow political abolitionism
at the polls, and repeal the unconstitutional and obnoxious laws
which, in the cause of " Personal Liberty," have been placed
on our statute books. I shall look with deep interest and not
without hope for a decided change in this relation.

Ever and truly your friend,
FRANKLIN PIERCE.

Hon. JEFF. DAVIS, Washington, D. C.

It was such assurances as those given in the above letter that
emboldened the Rebel leaders to war upon the government, and
there is a singular harmony between the assertions of Pierce
with regard to the course of events at the North and the views
of the Rebel newspapers at the South before the bombardment
of Fort Sumter. It will be recollected that they, too, predicted
civil war and bread riots at the North, showing that the assurances of Northern traitors had been credulously swallowed. — *Boston Journal: Supplement, September 25,* 1863.

The following from the " Boston Journal " of October 19th and
20th, 1863, presents a glimpse of the true attitude and character long possessed and maintained by this " Dear Friend "

to whom Mr. Pierce was then and appears yet to be so "ever and truly" attached.

MORE OF JEFF. DAVIS'S INTERCEPTED CORRESPONDENCE.— The following is a copy of a letter from Mason to Jeff. Davis, and was found among the intercepted correspondence of the latter.

SELMA, NEAR WINCHESTER, VA.,
September 30, 1856.

MY DEAR SIR : — I have a letter from Wise, of the 27th, full of spirit. He says the governments of North and South Carolinas and Louisiana have already agreed to the rendezvous at Raleigh, and others will. (This in your most private ear.) He says further that he had officially requested you to exchange with Virginia on fair terms of differences, percussion for flint muskets. Don't know the usage or power of department in such cases, but if it can be done soon by liberal constructions I hope you will accede. Was there not at the last session an appropriation for converting flint into percussion arms? If so, would it not furnish good reason for extending such facilities to the States? Virginia probably has more arms than the other Southern States, and would divide in case of need. In a letter yesterday to a committee in South Carolina, I gave it as my judgment, in the event of Fremont's election, the South should not pause, but proceed at once to immediate, absolute, and eternal separation. So I am a candidate for the first halter. Wise says his accounts from Philadelphia are cheering for old Buck in Pennsylvania. I hope they be not delusive. *Vale et salude.*

MASON'S LETTER. — This letter is one of the most valuable yet drawn from the treasure-house of the captured Jeff. Davis correspondence. It incontestably establishes, what has been extensively impressed upon the public mind, that the Southern leaders were prepared to ante-date the Rebellion four years, in case Fremont had been elected. They were resolved in 1856 to break up the Union the moment they could **not** hold its chief offices. The John Brown movement and other pretexts are thus proved to be utterly devoid of any foundation. The letter also shows that Floyd's thieving exploit with the public arms was not original with him, but had been hit upon four years earlier by Henry A. Wise, and commended by Mason to Jeff. Davis, Thus started and patronized, it was not likely to be forgotten whenever the time should come for putting it into execution.

D. (Page 301.)

The " New York Express " says there is not one word of truth in the statement about confessions, etc., and gives the following account of this victim to Rebel vengeance : —

Mr. Spencer Kellogg Brown, whose case is here mentioned, was the son of O. C. Brown of Jefferson county, New York. He enlisted in the army under General Lyon in 1861, and remained in active service until he was taken prisoner off Port Hudson, August 14th, 1862. He had been in the service of the government under Admiral Foote, and was on board the gunboat Essex, Commodore Porter, when that vessel committed such a havoc upon the Rebel ram, the Arkansas. He was captured as a prisoner of war while destroying a Rebel ferry-boat near Port Hudson, August 14th, and while under protection of a boat's crew of forty men, through whose cowardice, it is alleged, he was taken and made prisoner. There was an unnatural hatred felt toward all on board the Essex, and young Kellogg Brown was treated with such great indignity that Commodore Porter held five Rebel officers as hostages for his good treatment and release. On the solemn assurances of Ex-Governor Wickliffe of Louisiana that Brown should be treated as a prisoner of war, these five men were set free and have been exchanged, while a gallant officer is hung on the unfounded charge of being a spy. For over a year he has been kept as a close prisoner at Castle Thunder, in Richmond, and to-day his father, now in this city on business, hears through the Richmond papers, that his son was executed on Friday last.

What adds to this outrage and calamity, is the assurance of General Halleck, given as late as Monday last to the father of the murdered man, that his son should be protected, as there was no ground for his execution, and it was therefore impossible. Notice was given at once by a flag of truce that retaliation would follow such an act of brutality; but the assurance came too late, as the officer was executed on Friday last, three days before the interview.

———

E.

The following extracts of news, current while this volume is in press, verify the old proverb, " It is hard to teach old dogs new tricks; " also that other proverb of sacred origin, " Can the Ethiopian change his skin ? etc."

A special despatch to the " Chicago Tribune," dated at Indianapolis, Indiana, October 9th, says, —

" The Provost Marshal at Richmond, Indiana, arrested nineteen persons this morning, *all armed with revolvers, en route for Dayton, to vote for Vallandigham.* After their arrest, two of the party confessed the facts and stated that many more were expected to follow. They came to Richmond by different routes, and each had in his possesssion a rough map showing the different railroads leading through Indiana, to Dayton, Ohio. The leader of the party first gave his name as John Brown, but afterward said it was Webster Cassel, and that they all hailed from Chicago, Illinois."

The " Cincinnati Gazette " has a special despatch from Chicago which says, —

" The friends of Brough must be on the lookout for imported

votes. It is believed that a wide-spread scheme to colonize thousands of Copperheads from this State into Ohio is being carried out. The unlawful and nefarious work is being done under the auspices and management of the K. G. C.'s. The Copperhead organs of Chicago and Springfield advise Democrats to visit Ohio to see that Vallandigham has fair play. The nature of the visit and sort of fair play meant, your readers can guess. Many of those colonists from hereabout will strike for Cincinnati, where they expect to hide from sight and swear in their votes. The penalties for perjury or fear of detection will not restrain them from attemping to vote. Each is a repeater, and will vote early and often, but every town under Copperhead control will receive its share."

The "Philadelphia Bulletin," in commenting upon the result of the election, says, —

"The canvass for governor in Pennsylvania was one of the most spirited ever known. The Copperhead managers resorted to every trick, every deception, and every falsehood to carry the State for Woodward. He himself abandoned his former expressed opinions in order that he might obtain votes, and on the day before the election, Gen. McClellan, in a weak moment, was persuaded to abandon his very proper reserve and write a letter in favor of Woodward, which, it was hoped, would influence many votes. Colonizing was attempted on a stupendous scale, and even soldiers of the Rebel army were brought into Pennsylvania, placed on the assessors' rolls, and their taxes paid by Democratic politicians, in order to make a majority against Curtin. These, and all their other desperate expedients, have failed miserably. Andrew G. Curtin has been reëlected, and we believe that the legislature of the State will show a handsome Union majority."

If any one can show sufficient cause why a law should not be, first made, and then executed, defining as treason, and punishing with the death-penalty, every wilful corrupting of the civil

27

ballot, every counterfeiting of the national currency, and every wilful fraud on the national treasury, by making his reasons known, such person will relieve a somewhat prevalent and painful sense of deficiency in our national government.

———

F.

The proposition proposed to be supported by what is appended here, is, that the great majority of the masses of the Jackson-Buchanan party had been so acted on, by the principles and practices of that party, tending to deprave and despotize them, that up to the fall elections of 1863 they still adhered to the cause of Davis and their former chiefs. The following, from the "Boston Journal" of October 16th, demonstrates the real, which was the scarcely disguised, character of a man, of whose perjury and treason those masses previously had all the evidence of which the nature of the case admitted, and for whom they still cast their votes for governor in Ohio to the extent of 150,000.

We append a letter from Vallandigham which was recently captured in Tennessee among the baggage and private papers of the rebel officer to whom it was addressed. It was the most striking proof yet adduced of the treason of the man who has been so emphatically repudiated by the people of Ohio, although it is in perfect keeping with his whole course since the outbreak of the Rebellion. We can say that Ohio has made a decided and happy escape from being turned over into the hands of a traitor.

DEAR COLONEL:—Your kind note and invitation of yesterday was this morning handed me by your brother-in-law who will hand you this in return. It would give me much pleasure to visit you and your command before leaving the Confederacy, but it is now impossible to do so, as I have made arrangements to start this A. M. with the earliest train for Wilmington.

You surmise correctly, when you say that YOU BELIEVE ME TO BE THE FRIEND OF THE SOUTH IN HER STRUGGLE FOR FREEDOM. My feelings have been publicly expressed in my own country, in that quotation from Lord Chatham — "My Lords, *you cannot conquer America.*" There is not a drop of Puritan blood in my veins. I HATE, DESPISE AND DEFY THE TY- RANNICAL government which has sent me among you, for my opinion's sake. and shall NEVER GIVE IT MY SUPPORT IN ITS CRUSADE UPON YOUR INSTITUTIONS. But you are mistaken when you say there are but few such in the United States, North. THOUSANDS ARE THERE who would speak out but for the military despotism that strangles them.

Although the contest has been, and will continue to be, a bloody one, YOU HAVE BUT TO PERSEVERE and THE VICTORY WILL SURELY BE YOURS. YOU MUST STRIKE HOME! The de- fensive policy lengthens the contest. The shortest road to peace is the boldest one. YOU CAN HAVE YOUR OWN TERMS BY GAIN- ING THE BATTLE ON YOUR ENEMY'S SOIL.

Accept my kind regard for your personal welfare, and sin- cere thanks for your kind wishes in my behalf, and HOPING AND PRAYING FOR THE ULTIMATE CAUSE IN WHICH YOU ARE FIGHT- ING, believe me as ever your friend,

C. L. VALLANDIGHAM.

Col. D. D. INSHALL, 8th Ala. Vols.

A few weeks earlier, upwards of 50,000 of the same masses in Maine gave their votes for a gubernatorial candidate that stood pledged to coöperate with Vallandigham in carrying out his prin- ciples and policy ; and on the same day of the election in Ohio, 249,865 of the same depraved and despotized masses, out of a whole voting population of 515,003 in Pennsylvania, put forth their utmost effort to elect for that State a governor of the same principles and aims with Vallandigham.

Reverses to the national arms, or the desperate exertions of their old leaders, were and still are, liable from the old stock of that party to raise those numbers to ruling majorities in either and each of the above-named States, as they did last year in New York and Indiana.

Thus near had Democracy in America, and the last hope of a tyrant-ridden world, been brought to extinction, by the operation of the principles and practices of the above-named political party, acting on the masses of the population that had been directly and fully under their influence.

In the light of recent developments, we will here glance at another source of peril to the same cause that arose from a somewhat different quarter. The following, from the " Portland Courier " of October 22d, 1863, is a fit and reliable commentary on the letter that succeeds : —

Everybody who reads the "Boston Journal," knows that Burleigh, who writes the New York and Saratoga gossip for that paper, has always been partial to General McClellan, and has written many sentences in his favor. The late letter of General McClellan, however, has wrought a change, and Burleigh speaks of it as follows : —

The political letter of Gen. McClellan, intending to aid in the defeat of Governor Curtin of Pennsylvania, has been read with profound sorrow by thousands of his friends. When it was announced that such a letter had been written by him, few believed it. His long silence under the heavy charges preferred against him by the Congressional Committee — his patient waiting under what many supposed were wrongs inflicted upon him — his manly submission to the decree which condemned him to semi-disgrace — the belief that in due time he would vindicate himself — gave him a strong hold on the public sympathy. His silence when his military ability and honor were assailed, and the promptness with which he defends his political opinions are not the least remarkable things in this letter. But the character of the letter itself has probably done the work for Gen. McClellan, It justifies what his enemies have long charged upon him in his method of conducting the war. He comes, uncalled for, a volunteer witness in Court to aid his enemies, and to enable them to do what, without his efforts, they could never have done. He shows that his heart was never in the war ; that he intended to carry on a defensive, and not an offensive war ; that he would defend the capital and all the soil held by the loyal North, beat back the Rebels, in every attempt to advance out of the seceding States, to hold them in check till the Northern elections should change the administration, and so secure peace by compromise, and not by the sword. The letter justifies the President in the removal of McClellan from the command of the army. All testimony concedes that McClellan was a great favorite with the President. While his headquarters were in Washington the President saw him every day, and passed most of his evenings with him. He generally called him " Georgie," and was tenderly attached to him. To give him up cost him a long and painful struggle. It was not until he was thoroughly convinced that the policy of Gen. McClellan. which he would not change, was irreconcilable with the preservation of our national life, that he gave the order for his removal. Such a letter as this of McClellan would have killed Junius.

ORANGE, NEW JERSEY, Oct. 12th, 1863.

HON. CHARLES J. BIDDLE.

DEAR SIR : — My attention has been called to an article in the "Philadelphia Press," asserting that I had written to the managers of the Democratic meeting at Allentown, disapproving of the objects of the meeting, and that if I voted and spoke, it would be in favor of Governor Curtin.

I am informed that similar assertions have been made throughout the State. It has been my earnest endeavor heretofore to avoid participation in party politics, and I had determined to ad-

27*

here to this course ; but it is obvious that I cannot long maintain silence under such misrepresentations. I therefore request you to deny that I have written any such letter, or entertained any such views as those attributed to me in the " Philadelphia Press."

I desire to state clearly and distinctly that having some few days ago had a full conversation with Judge Woodward, I find that our views agree, and I regard his election as Governor of Pennsylvania called for by the interest of the nation.

I understand Judge Woodward to be in favor of the prosecuion of the war with all the means at the command of the loyal States, until the military power of the Rebellion is destroyed.

I understand him to be of the opinion that while war is waged with all possible decision and energy, the policy directing it should be in consonance with the principles of humanity and civilization, working no injury to private rights and property not demanded by military necessity and recognized by military law among civilized nations. And finally,

I understand him to agree with me in the opinion that the sole great objects of the war are the restoration of the Union of the nation, the preservation of the Constitution and the supremacy of the laws of the country.

Believing that our opinions entirely agree upon these points, I would, were it in my power, give to Judge Woodward my voice and my vote.

I am, very respectfully, yours,
GEORGE B. McCLELLAN.

Three historic characters here present themselves. Judge Woodward, Gen. McClellan, and President Lincoln.

Judge Woodward, but for his insignificance, might with propriety be termed James Buchanan No. 2, and appears justly to merit all the increase of odium that attaches to the character that term describes at the present, in comparison with a former day. There appears to have been scarcely anything, short of the overt act of treason which would have condemned him to the gallows, which he has not done, in the fore-front of the Rebel sympathizers, to aid the traitor's cause. Of what he had said and done in this direction, he had swallowed, contradicted, and undone nothing, more than would have been swallowed, contradicted, and undone by any man of his political school, to gain the votes of men less traitorous than himself.

All this was perfectly known to McClellan. It was known to him that the positions occupied by Woodward and Vallandigham, and the measures resorted to to sustain these positions at the same time in the several States of Ohio and Pennsylvania, were substantially parallel.* And yet McClellan could not restrain himself from coming out at the last decisive hour, in a carefully worded but desperate effort to throw Pennsylvania and the Union back into the hands of such men as Judge Woodward,† James Buchanan, Isaac Toucey, John B. Floyd, Franklin Pierce, Jefferson Davis, and to subject Pennsylvania and the Union again to the operation of the political principles, which these names represent.

From July 27th, 1861, to November 9th, 1862, George B. McClellan commanded the army of the Potomac, and, during several months of this time, the armies of the United States. When first called to that position of unparalleled importance and

---

* See Appendix D.

† Judge Woodward, the opposition candidate for Governor of Pennsylvania, has been convicted, on the strongest authority, of having publicly declared in the spring of 1861 that if these States are to be separated he hoped Pennsylvania would go with the South, which was then about to take arms to break down the government.

Mr. George W. Hart of Philadelphia, always a Democrat hitherto, says in a letter that he travelled three days with Judge Woodward, the Democratic candidate for Governor of Pennsylvania, and heard him say often that this " was an unconstitutional war and an abolition war, and that he had no interest whatever in the result, let this result be what it might; that it was a contest in which the North could gain neither credit nor honor, and this he believed would be the verdict of history." — *Boston Journal, Sept.* 26 *and Oct.* 3*d*, 1863.

responsibility, he was hailed with a universal welcome. The
talents he displayed in organizing a vast army, and in inspiring
his men with hope and confidence, commanded universal admiration. The loyal millions breathed freer at his advent, introduced
and endorsed as he was by the retiring veteran of peerless renown, who had preceded him. The friends of Free-government
throughout the world were glad that their cause had fallen into so
able hands.

Had the sun stood still, and all human events and actions suspended progress, at the point at which General McClellan matured the recruiting and organizing of his army, then might his
name have remained illustrious, — at least, with some dawning
beams about it. But on no other condition could he be spared
the necessity of acting out, on a transcendently important and
conspicuous arena, the principles of his heart.

What was the record? Delay in advancing to Manassas —
defeated by Fabian tactics — delay at Yorktown — 80,000 men
consumed by the heat of summer in the malarious swamps of the
Chickahominy, and in the overwhelming assaults which his de-
lays obtained for him — Pope and his army immolated at the second battle of Bull Run, through the obstinate tardiness, or wilful
refusal of McClellan and his crony commanders, to forward the
needed succor as commanded. Next came the terrible day of
Antietam, on which McClellan refrained from firing a shot, more
than was indispensable to prevent Baltimore, Philadelphia, and
Washington from falling immediately into the enemy's hands.

What does all this mean ? — the astonished, bewildered, disheartened and stricken loyalists in this country, and the friends
of liberal government throughout the world, have been asking ;
and never, till George B. McClellan signed and sent that letter,
to turn if possible the Pennsylvania election in favor of the Rebel
sympathizers,* has light enough been accumulated to enable any

* PHILADELPHIA, Nov. 11. Judges Lourie, Woodward and Thompson of
the Supreme Court of Pennsylvania, in session at Pittsburg, being a majori-

one who was at liberty to do so, reliably to interpret this page of appalling history.

ty of the Court, gave a decision on Monday relative to certain drafted men, in effect declaring the conscription act unconstitutional.

THE RIOTS IN THE COAL DISTRICTS. — A special correspondent of the Philadelphia Press writes from Mauch Chunk, Pa., on the 7th instant, as follows: —

"Several accounts appeared during the last few days in Philadelphia and New York papers of the 'riots' in this region, and the murder of Mr. G. K. Smith, one of our best and most valuable citizens. The accounts given are, as far as they go, substantially correct. The murders committed, however, are not 'riots,' but the work of assassins, extensively organized throughout the coal region; and the leading Copperheads are the chief instigators.

" The murderers are all Irish, organized under the name of 'Buckshots' for the avowed purpose of resisting the draft. They number probably several thousand in the mines of Beaver Meadow, Coleraine, Jeanesville, Hazleton, Audenried, Yorktown, Frenchtown, Spring Mountain and Mount Pleasant, They are all armed either with shot-guns, rifles, muskets, or revolvers. The most notorious Copperheads of our place counselled them to arm themselves 'to defend their liberties,' and to 'resist the tyranny of the Lincoln despotism.' The beasts, duped by these demagogues, declare their determination to drive out of the mines every one who is not of their own stripe; and a number of Welshmen, Englishmen, Protestant Irish, Germans, and Americans have been waylaid and murdered by them during the last two or three months. About two months ago, one of these Buckshots was arrested near Beaver Meadow, and lodged in our jail, on a charge of assault and battery with intent to kill. On the following night, over one hundred Buckshots marched into town well armed, arriving here about one o'clock in the morning, surrounded the jail, and rescued the prisoner. No effort was made by the civil authorities to arrest the offenders, although the grand jury, last month, presented the names of a number of persons who participated in the outrage. The district attorney, being of the most malignant stamp of Copperheads, refused, and continues to refuse, any steps calculated to bring these villains to justice. The high sheriff of the county, it is believed, would prefer doing his duty; but he being in the Copperhead boat cannot do so. He has made no effort to raise a *posse comitatus* for the arrest of these or any other outlaws in our county. Even one of the associate judges of our court, and leading officer of one of the most prosperous and respectable local corporations, it is said, discountenanced any effort to arrest 'Buckshots,' simply because they (the Democracy) 'need their votes, and must not offend them.'

" Thus encouraged by our local authorities, these outlaws frequently declared their determination to not only kill every officer who would undertake

In the war of the American Revolution, Great Britain failed to subdue the revolted colonies for lack of military commanders who heartily undertook the task assigned them. The policy of McClellan and of the political school to which he lent himself appears to have been, to defeat the efforts of the present administration through the operation of a similar cause, to keep the losses, exhaustion, and bloodshed of the present war about equally divided between the two contending sections, call it a drawn game, and submit the questions at issue back to the operation of the same causes that first brought them under the arbitration of the sword! In other words, that policy was, so to conduct the existing war, that its cost, its sufferings, and its slaughtered thousands, should just avail as a judicious blood-letting to reduce the Southern leaders to the position they occupied before they bolted from their fellow partisans at the Charleston Convention, and thus enable the old political party to revalidate its old usurpation, and handle its old opponents with all the greater ease by as much as they had been impoverished and decimated in the war!!

Let him, if such an one there be, who is competent to the task, do justice to the events, and fitly characterize the actors presented on this page of history!

If General George B. McClellan failed to fulfil the expectations entertained of him as Commander-in-Chief of the Union forces, or as Commander of the magnificent army of the Potomac, those expectations appear to have been disappointed, not because he lacked the power, but because he lacked the will, that was requisite for their fulfilment. The reticence with which he suppressed his real sentiments and aims, and the successful address with which he kept the administration at his chariot-

to enforce the draft, but also to put out of the way every one suspected of sympathy with the government. They openly declare now their determination to secure entire control of all the mines, and to stop the shipment of coal, and thus deprive the navy of this indispensable article." — *Boston Journal, Nov.* 12th, 1863.

wheel, while he carried those sentiments into effect, and advanced those aims towards their final achievement, on so vast a scale, indoctrinating his generals and attaching to himself the rank and file of his army, prove General McClellan to be well endowed with executive ability to accomplish anything that he has the moral elevation to attempt.

The peril that arose, to the cause of popular government in general and to the United States in particular, from the course of General McClellan while in command of United States forces, may be traced to its primal source in the causes that had despotized the masses of the Jackson-Buchanan party. He is an eminent individual specimen of what elsewhere appears in depraved masses. But it is another source of peril displayed in this connection, to which we here glance briefly.

Whatever was wanting in tenderness was made up in strength, in the composition of that man who could see more than one hundred thousand of his fellow-citizens consumed before his face in fifteen months by disease and casualties, from the ranks under his command, — to say nothing of the nearly equal waste that occurred simultaneously just across the line in his front, — and persist in regarding the whole as an ordinary, and perhaps-to-be-repeated sacrifice to the Moloch of his political party; and, at the end put forth his earnest effort to prevent the disaster from availing for any higher end. Far less extensive views than General McClellan had, of the disaster and sorrow brought upon their countrymen by the nefarious originators of this war, had availed to turn the judgments and the hearts of tens of thousands of McClellan's fellow-partisans who went into the war as honest and as earnest in their allegiance to his political party as himself. But out of it all McClellan came with an obdurate few, unable to see any object to be accomplished by the incomputable costs, higher or holier than the restoration of the policy of Pierce, Buchanan, and Toucey with its attendant benefits, to "the interest of the nation" — unable to aspire to any higher or holier political

vocation than, with men like these, to grind in the prison-
house of that foul sect, with a view to keeping in subjection
under them all those of their remaining fellow-citizens who aspire
to the attainment of a political destiny less ignominious than
their own. "Join our political party, and follow the leaders or
be left out in the cold " — " to the victors belong the spoils " —
is the language with which they prepare to greet us, the moment
that any kind or amount of political fraud or villany enables
them to elect the candidate of their nominating.

That the inaugural address of President Lincoln seemed defi-
cient in boldness, was attributed at the time to a sagacious, but
not the less decided, prudence. That no prompt, decisive steps
were taken to arrest the progress of insurgent fortifications
around Charleston, and to reinforce Fort Sumter, sickened the
loyal heart. That seventeen months of the war, with their slaughter and their cost, went by without the administration having
adopted any principle or policy that appeared adequate to secure
a beneficial result, or even to end the fight, appalled the thought-
ful friends of popular government in this country and in Europe.
It was presumed that the diplomatic member of President Lincoln's Cabinet, with undue influence was inducing his chief to
found his plans and expectations, not so much on the rock of
any particular civil truths or principles, as on the fathomless
abyss of diplomacy. That President Lincoln, during much of this
time was spending his evenings in the fascinating company of a
man, who, after passing through the war-experience of that com-
manding general, would put his name to such a letter as was addressed to Charles J. Biddle on the eve of the late Pennsylvania election, was a calamity, a tremendous peril, — a verging
of the car of Liberty along the brink of chaos, — which freedom's friends at the time were spared the misery of contemplating. Now that we see it in the light of accomplished facts,
it reminds one of Marshal Grouchy on the eve of Waterloo, in
conference with the emissary of the Allies. To subject him-

self and his country's cause to the effect of such a perilous temptation displayed President Lincoln's sad trait. To extricate himself and his cause from the impending ruin, almost unharmed —to rebound into the line of clear, decisive, necessary, and gloriously successful policy which his former fascinator is now struggling to resist, displays President Lincoln's redeeming excellence in its tardy but ultimate ascendency, — displays perhaps the "grace of God that was given unto him" in answer to the prayers of God's imperilled, believing people.

G.

In a letter to the General Assembly of Ohio, acknowledging the receipt of a resolution of thanks from that body to the Army of the Cumberland and its officers, Gen. Rosecrans employs the following emphatic language : —

" This is indeed a war for the maintenance of the Constitution and the laws — nay, for national existence against those who have despised our honest friendship, deceived our just hopes, and driven us to defend our country and our homes. By foul and wilful slanders on our motives and intentions, persistently repeated, they have arrayed against us our own fellow-citizens, bound to us by the triple ties of consanguinity, geographical position, and commercial interest.

" Let no man among us be base enough to forget this, or fool enough to trust an oligarchy of traitors to their friends, to civil liberty, and human freedom. Voluntary exiles from home and friends, for the defence and safety of all, we long for the time when gentle peace shall again spread her wings over our land ; but we know no such blessing is possible while the unjust and arbitrary power of the Rebel leaders confronts and threatens us, Crafty as the fox, cruel as the tiger, they cried ' No coercion,' while preparing to strike us. Bully-like they proposed to fight us because they said they could whip five to one ; and now,

28

when driven back, they whine out ' no invasion,' and promise us of the West permission to navigate the Mississippi, if we will be ' good boys,' and do as they bid us.

" Whenever they have the power, they drive before them into their ranks the Southern people, and they would also drive us. Trust them not. 'Were they able, they would invade and destroy us without mercy. Absolutely assured of these things, I am amazed that any one could think of ' peace on any terms.' He who entertains the sentiment is fit only to be a slave ; he who utters it at this time is, moreover, a traitor to his country, who deserves the scorn and contempt of all honorable men. When the power of the unscrupulous Rebel leaders is removed, and the people are free to consider and act for their own interests, which are common with ours under this government, there will be no great difficulty in fraternization." — *Boston Journal, Feb.* 16*th,* 1863

Of the above extract from Gen. Rosecrans's letter it may be said that an equal amount of sagacious statesmanship and patriotic faithfulness has not been expressed in the same space, — has not been compressed into any one document, — (it may almost be said) has not been expressed in all the documents and speeches which the present war has brought out. It presents Gen. Rosecrans himself, simply, unsubverted, unsophisticated, an American Democrat in the true and proper meaning of the term.

The following, translated from the "*Courrier des Etats Unis,*" which professes to have obtained it from a Cincinnati correspondent, represents Gen. Rosecrans in the shape to which he would be reduced, and in the attitude and light in which he would be placed by his spiritual advisers, the emissaries of the " decrepit giant " who, as seen from Bedford jail two hundred years ago, was " biting his nails " for lack of power to commit the devastation he desired ; provided said emissaries succeed to their minds in accomplishing the mission on which they have been sent.

" Persons who are on intimate terms with Gen. Rosecrans de-clare that he is greatly discouraged about the war.   This is not because he considers the Southern armies invincible, but because he believes that the seceded States can never be brought back by the rigorous policy which the government has adopted.   He has never taken any part in the proceedings of Andrew Johnson, the military governor of Tennessee, who has succeeded in converting to Secession all people who had any hopes of the Union.   Him-self perfectly disinterested, he looks with disgust upon the shameful traffic which is going on under the mask of patriotism. When he looks around him, he sees men moved by all sorts of motives, more or less decent, except honor and the love of coun-try.   Some are fighting from ambition, others from avarice ; to the latter the conquest of country means only pillage and cheap cotton ; the former are jealous of their superiors and their equals, and are delighted with any reverse which may overtake them.

" Profoundly honest and religious, Rosecrans regards these spectacles with bitter aversion.   His religious feelings have grown upon him in proportion to the excesses and intrigues which he is impotent to prevent; and, in mystical hopes of another world, he seeks relief from the corruptions of the present.   He no longer fights with any ardor, but simply from a sense of duty, consider-ing each victory a useless waste of blood.   He has no confi-dence in his successes, considering that they are followed by the swoop of birds of prey whose rapacity makes hopeless the pacifi-cation of the country. . . . . All these details come to me from a person very dear to Rosecrans, to whom the General wrote that he saw in the defeat of Chickamauga the finger of God."—*Bos-ton Journal, Oct. 27th,* 1863.

TO THE BAFFLED DESPOTS OF THE SOUTH.

YE are going down whence ye rose at first,
From the face of the Land your lust has cursed ;
From the light of your hope, and your lied-for crown,
In darkness and blood ye are going down.

Ye chose you a corner whereon to rear
The throne of your power, a realm of fear ;
Ye swore to rule with a despot's rod
O'er the Land, the People, and the Saints of God.

The sable sons of a heathen race
Long bowed to your mandates with abject grace ;
And your slaveless kindred, bereft of dower,
Have quailed and bled 'neath your crushing power,

Till the voice of their blood, from the wreaking sod,
Has entered the ears of an incensed God,
And beneath the blight of his burning frown,
To the despot's doom ye are going down.

" Hell from beneath is moved for thee,*
    The despot dead thy coming greet, —
' Art thou also become weak as we ? '
    The defunct kings of the nations shriek.

" In glory each in his house they lie,
    But thou, cast out, art keenly scanned,
And trampled down by each passer-by,
    Because thou hast destroyed thy land.

" The whole earth is at rest once more,
    The trees and the fields rejoice 'gainst thee."
And wide and deep as Ocean's roar,
    Goes up the song of slaves set free.

The despots slain mid Freedom's Home,
    The boldest, bloodiest of their kind,
We trust may be the last that come,
    Their shackles on our limbs to bind.

JANUARY 16, 1864.

* Isaiah, xlv.

www.ingramcontent.com/pod-product-compliance
Lightning Source LLC
Chambersburg PA
CBHW060512030726
47498CB00004B/923